T0128108

Divine Wisdom and Knowledge

*I have realized that to fear God and keep
his commandments ensures divine wisdom
with an inheritance from the Lord God.*

DAVID O. INYANG

authorHOUSE®

AuthorHouse™
1663 Liberty Drive
Bloomington, IN 47403
www.authorhouse.com
Phone: 1 (800) 839-8640

© 2018 David O. Inyang. All rights reserved.

No part of this book may be reproduced, stored in a retrieval system, or transmitted by any means without the written permission of the author.

Published by AuthorHouse 08/02/2018

ISBN: 978-1-5462-3597-2 (sc)
ISBN: 978-1-5462-3596-5 (e)

Library of Congress Control Number: 2018904227

Print information available on the last page.

Any people depicted in stock imagery provided by Getty Images are models, and such images are being used for illustrative purposes only.
Certain stock imagery © Getty Images.

This book is printed on acid-free paper.

Because of the dynamic nature of the Internet, any web addresses or links contained in this book may have changed since publication and may no longer be valid. The views expressed in this work are solely those of the author and do not necessarily reflect the views of the publisher, and the publisher hereby disclaims any responsibility for them.

all bible scriptures taken from KJV

CONTENTS

DEDICATION

This piece of work is dedicated to all those that aspire for excellence, and strive towards mastery of life and perfection in life.

In Memoriam

In memory of the humble, meek and selfless apostle of Christ, **Late Pastor Eyo Edet Okon** who was fondly called **Akamba Ete**. May the Lord God bless his gentle soul eternally, Amen.

BASCO STUDIOS
LATE PASTOR EYO EDET OKON (1914 – 2010)
First National President,
The Apostolic Church of Nigeria.

ℙROLOGUE

It is an immense privilege to present to you one of the excellencies of God and priceless treasures in life, which is the wisdom and knowledge of God. Passionate seekers of truth always find it as necessity is the mother of all invention and innovation. It must have been your dire need to acquire divine wisdom, know God, overcome fear and lack, do great exploits, and attain lofty heights. It is not by chance that you are reading this book but God made it possible, so that you can have the grace of God to be wise, hardworking, creative and prosperous.

The whole attack of the Devil is aimed at the mind of man. The onslaught may comprise insanity, foolishness, ignorance, wrong philosophies, false doctrines, distorted psyche, perversions, misconceptions, fear (phobia), taboo, superstitions, influence of hard drugs (sedatives, anesthetics, tranquilizers and other mind-blowing drug).

In his book *Psychotherapy*, Martin Sphepard opined that for greater mental development one needs to improve upon his standards of ethics, goals and spiritual values. Our minds must be renewed continuously and daily in Christ Jesus. In addition, one should be committed to seeking divine knowledge, truth, understanding and love.

This is a contribution to the science of the mind from a biblical perspective. It may not be as comprehensive and elaborate as that of King Solomon. I also applied my heart:

> To know wisdom
> And to search out wisdom
> And to seek out wisdom,

And to know the reason of all things
And to know the wickedness of folly,
Even to understand foolishness and madness. (Eccl. 7:25)

I realized that to fear God and keep his commandments ensures divine wisdom with an inheritance from the Lord God.

David Inyang
Calabar, Nigeria
December, 2017

Acknowledgements

I wish to acknowledge all authors and teachers whom I have benefited in no small measure all through my search for divine wisdom and knowledge. Prominent amongst them are Watchman Nee, A.W. Tozer, and Finis Jennings Dake. I acknowledge Merriam–Webster dictionary and thesaurus for all definitions used in this book.

Above all, I magnify the most high God for who He is and His love on all His creation and His inspiration to mankind. I also express my heartfelt gratitude to all members of my families, my mother, my lovely sisters, my dear wife, Akamba and our three children-David, Daniel and Josepha for their breathe-taking fun-filled trouble.

I acknowledge my teacher, Eld. Victor Ironbar, whose idea during an annual youth seminar led to the conception of this book. I also thank my good friends especially Sir Gbolahan Olayomi, Pastor Dominic Efanga, Prof. Daniel Owu, Ps. (Dr) Eteng Etobe, Ps (Dr) Patrick Ene-Okon, Ps (Barr) Edem Ekong and Prof Eyo Mensah for their critical discussions, editorial comments and support.

I am sincerely grateful to Basco Photo Studio for the portrait. I appreciate Amaka, Ndiana and Comfort for typing and formatting the manuscript, and Geotetrax Services for the publication of this book. All Bible citations are from King James Version of Dake's Bible and e-sword Bible software.

I pray that the Most High God should bless everyone including my readers and those I have failed to acknowledge here.

David O. Inyang.

Part I

Introduction

Overview of Divine Wisdom and Knowledge

God cherishes saints who requests for wisdom and understanding as Solomon did. King Solomon requested of God an understanding heart to judge the people that he may discern between good and bad (**1 King 3: 9**). The request for wisdom and understanding pleased God (**1 King 3: 10**) and God granted unto him a wise and understanding heart, with riches and honour that he did not request for (**1 King 3:12- 13**). God granted unto him understanding to discern judgement (**1 King 4: 29-30**). Since Solomon did not express selfishness in his petition to God by asking for long life, riches or lives of his enemies instead he asked for wisdom and understanding. This request of wisdom and understanding pleased God, he added unto Solomon riches and honour (**I King 3: 10-14**).

*I King 3:10 -And the speech pleased the Lord, that Solomon had asked this thing. **I King 3:11** -And God said unto him, Because thou hast asked this thing, and hast not asked for thyself long life; neither hast asked riches for thyself, nor hast asked the life of thine enemies; but hast asked for thyself understanding to discern judgment; **I King 3:12** -Behold, I have done according to thy words: lo, I have given thee a wise and an understanding heart; so that there was none like thee before thee, neither after thee shall any arise like unto thee. **I King 3:13** -And I have also given thee that which thou hast not asked, both riches, and honour: so that there shall not be any among the kings like unto thee all thy days. **I King 3:14** -And if thou wilt walk in my ways, to keep my statutes and my commandments, as thy father David did walk, then I will lengthen thy days.*

The Lord God, by his creative wisdom hath founded the earth and the heavens (***Prov.3:19**-The LORD by wisdom hath founded the earth; by* *understanding hath he established the heavens. **Prov. 3:20** -By his knowledge the depths are broken up, and the clouds drop down the dew).* Creative wisdom or creativity has its source in God. It is readily available to men that are holy and consecrated unto God *(Ps 15:2; Ps 24: 3-4) and* have the Spirit of God.

Unfortunately, many people are without divine wisdom and knowledge because the world and the Devil seek to make the children of God ignorant, senseless, mad, foolish, confused and devoid of wisdom and knowledge of God. The Devil and his agents prefer or want the children of God to be inert, spineless or passive (i.e. lacking will power) in order to manipulate, use and oppress them.

The word of God says that the thief comes to steal, kill and destroy (**Jn 10:10**-*The thief cometh not, but for to steal, and to kill, and to destroy: I am come that they might have life, and that they might have it more abundantly).* The evil ones seek to destroy the mind, darken the light (star), blind the eyes, weaken one's strength just like Samson and deprive one of his freedom and livelihood in order to achieve the sole aim of stealing, killing and destroying.

Verily, God desires every saint to know the whole counsel of God *(Act 20:27)* as our Lord himself declared unto his friends all what he heard from God the Father since it is not good for a man to be without knowledge *(**Prov 19:2**-Also, that the soul be without knowledge, it is not good; and he that hasteth with his feet sinneth).*

This is the reason why one must strive for the excellency of divine wisdom and knowledge. The Devil wages war against the children of God and seeks ways to wear out the saints of the Most High *(I Pet. 5:8- Be sober, be vigilant; because your adversary the devil, as a roaring lion, walketh about, seeking whom he may devour; **Dan 7:25**-And he shall speak great words against the most High, and shall wear out the saints of the most High, and think to change times and laws).*

It is my sincere desire that you should study this book with every scriptural passage cited for deeper understanding of the excellency of divine wisdom and knowledge. I dare to say that the human mind is the greatest asset that a man has and must be developed and protected with divine guidance and wisdom. The extent of divine wisdom and knowledge is influenced by the extent of the love of God. The evil ones seek to influence, possess, manipulate, and control one's mind.

God wants every saint to control his mind in the right way according to divine will but the devil wants to control man's mind, his will, memory and conscience.

The universe was created perfect by the Supreme Being (**Gen. 1**) but human beings in the world, through depravity, have made it extremely wicked and violent. That is why we need the wisdom of God to survive and to do great exploits. We have to be cunning as a serpent and harmless as a dove (*Mat 10:16 - Behold, I send you forth as sheep in the midst of wolves: be ye therefore wise as serpents, and harmless as doves).* The importance of divine wisdom in the well-being and preservation of the sheep or the flock of God is reiterated emphatically here.

We are like sheep amongst the wolves, and on our own, we do not possess the facilities and the faculties to wage war or fight against the wild and experienced wolves. It is very pitiful that God's children are not taught the intrigues and maneuvers of the world *(Luk 16:8)* and how to be overcomers. *For whatsoever is born of God overcometh the world: and this is the victory that overcometh the world, our faith. (1Jn 5:4-5) Who is he that overcometh the world, but he that believeth that Jesus is the Son of God?).* Our faith in God must be strongly built in the word and knowledge of God. Every saint is warned strictly not to learn the evil ways of the world, in order to overcome the world. *Jer. 10:2 Say "Thus saith the LORD, Learn not the way of the heathen, and be not dismayed at the signs of heaven; for the heathen are dismayed at them".*

Due to this lack of knowledge which results in faithlessness and passivity of man's will, the work of God suffers setbacks. Ignorance is the cause of passivity of man's will. And passivity of the mind also gives way to the Devil to control (*Spiritual Man* - Watchman Nee). The worst state of a man is being besides himself thereby allowing the extraneous spirit or the Devil to take full control of his entire being. In this state, man's spirit has been subdued and relegated to a secondary position by another spirit, from whom his spirit/being obeys unquestionably.

Our children must be wise, knowledgeable, aggressive, assertive and adventurous for good and for greatness in order to be "more than conquerors" in Christ Jesus. This attitude in Christians will create opportunities for God to manifest his glory and might in the world. No saint should be like a horse that lacks understanding *(Ps 32:9- Be ye not as the horse, or as the mule, which have no understanding: whose mouth must be held in with bit and bridle, lest they come near unto thee.).* The scripture does not state what attributes are exemplified by the horse / mule that consider it to be amongst the dumb animals of the world. It is probably its stubbornness to charge into raging calamity, and war, just like the foolish man that walks into calamity headlong. Secondly, it may be his willingness to meddle in strife, war, or affair that is not its own in contrast to a wise man.

We must seek divine wisdom and knowledge as men of understanding *('The heart of him that hath understanding seeketh knowledge: but the mouth of fools feedeth on foolishness. **Prov. 15:14).***

In order to achieve this purpose, I am presenting to you our Lord Jesus Christ as the embodiment of all the treasures of wisdom and knowledge:

Col 2:3 *-In whom are hid all the treasures of wisdom and knowledge;* **I Cor.1:24;** But *unto them which are called, both Jews and Greeks, Christ the power of God, and the wisdom of God;* **1Cor 1:30** *But of him are ye in Christ Jesus, who of God is made unto us wisdom, and righteousness, and sanctification, and redemption.*

Every saint who is in Christ Jesus, should be a custodian of divine wisdom and knowledge since he is endued with the spirit of wisdom and understanding *(**Isa 11:2-** And the spirit of the LORD shall rest upon him, the spirit of wisdom and understanding, the spirit of counsel and might, the spirit of knowledge and of the fear of the LORD).* He is not meant to be ignorant or foolish. The word of God enjoins us to learn divine wisdom (**Prov. 1:2-7**) and have the mind of Christ (***Phil. 2:5** - Let this mind be in you, which was also in Christ Jesus).*

Prov 1:2-*To know wisdom and instruction; to perceive the words of understanding;* **Prov 1:3-** *To receive the instruction of wisdom, justice, and judgment, and equity;* **Prov 1:4-***To give subtilty to the simple, to the young man knowledge and discretion.* **Prov 1:5** *A wise man will hear, and will increase learning; and a man of understanding shall attain unto wise counsels:***Prov 1:6** *-To understand a proverb, and the interpretation; the words of the wise, and their dark sayings.* **Prov 1:7** *- The fear of the LORD is the beginning of knowledge: but fools despise wisdom and instruction.*

When one fears God and walks uprightly, he understands and finds knowledge of God. Every saint is required to have the knowledge and wisdom of God (**Prov. 2:5-11**). *Then shalt thou understand the fear of the LORD, and find the knowledge of God.* **Prov 2:6** *For the LORD giveth wisdom: out of his mouth cometh knowledge and understanding.* **Prov 2:7** *He layeth up sound wisdom for the righteous: he is a buckler to them that walk uprightly.* **Prov 2:8** *He keepeth the paths of judgment, and preserveth the way of his saints.* **Prov 2:9** *Then shalt thou understand righteousness, and judgment, and equity; yea, every good path.* **Prov 2:10** *When wisdom entereth into thine heart, and knowledge is pleasant unto thy soul;* **Prov 2:11**-*Discretion shall preserve thee, understanding shall keep thee)* God is a God of knowledge.

(**I Sam. 2:3** - *Talk no more so exceeding proudly; let not arrogancy come out of your mouth: for the LORD is a God of knowledge, and by him actions are weighed;* **Job 36:4b** - *For truly my words shall not be false: he that is perfect in knowledge is with thee.*

The knowledge and wisdom of God should propel saints to excellence, effectiveness, and greatness but not mediocrity, complacency and subservience. Every saint should endeavor to unleash his full human potentials and live unto the fullness of God in him (**Eph.1:23**-*Which is his body, the fulness of him that filleth all in all. And to know the love of Christ, which passeth knowledge, that ye might be filled with all the fulness of God;* **Eph.4:13**. *Till we all come in the unity of the faith, and of the knowledge of the Son of God, unto a perfect man, unto the measure of the stature of the fulness of Christ;* **Col.1:19**. *For it pleased the Father that in him should all fulness dwell;* **Col 2:9** -*For in him dwelleth all the fulness of the Godhead bodily;* **Jn 1:16**.-*And of his fulness have all we received, and grace for grace.*

Every saint has already received the full potential of Christ in him or her and must develop it to its fullness and exhibit it in his or her daily living. (**Eph.4:14** - *That we henceforth be no more children, tossed to and fro, and carried about with every wind of doctrine, by the sleight of men, and cunning craftiness, whereby they lie in wait to deceive).* Every saint should pray hard, read hard and work hard as a well-equipped saint. He is to mind his business (**I Thess 4:11**) and judiciously manage his time, energy and resources to avoid wastage because these gifts of ours are expended in trickles continuously on a daily basis which add up to unquantifiable amount in the long run.

Meaning of Wisdom and Knowledge

Firstly, we must ask ourselves some pertinent questions: What is wisdom? What is knowledge? What is understanding?

Wisdom is the ability to make sensible judgments and decisions, especially on the basis of one's knowledge and experience; prudence and common sense. Wisdom is the ability which enables men to judge what are the best ends and the best means of attaining them (Dake's Bible). Wisdom is displayed in saints by the hearing and doing of the word of God (**Matt 7:24**-*Therefore whosoever heareth these sayings of mine, and doeth them, I will liken him unto a wise man, which built his house upon a rock*).

Knowledge: According to Merriam-Webster dictionary, knowledge is the awareness or consciousness, understanding, or information one has acquired through learning or experience.

Understanding is one's perception or interpretation of information received. (Teacher's note: illustrate or describe the differences in magnitude of heat and fire using candle, fireplace, fire incident, furnace, forest fire, and inferno to enhance the perception or understanding of children). Only an experienced child can really appreciate or perceive the extent of heat and the magnitude of fire in the description of an inferno as two trucks fully loaded with gasoline collide and burst into flames.

The word '**discernment**' has a close relationship with the word 'understanding'. Closely related to understanding are words such as **prudence** and **discretion**. **Prov.16:21** and **Hosea 14:9** illustrate this closeness in meaning of these words: *Prov 16:21*-*The wise in heart shall be called prudent: and the sweetness of the lips increaseth learning*; **Hos 14:9**-*Who **is wise,** and he shall understand these **things?** prudent, and he shall know them? for the ways of the LORD **are** right, and the just shall walk in them: but the transgressors shall fall therein.*

Excellence is exceptional quality or worth of something; extremely good and complete without flaws – perfect. **Excellency** is the state of being excellent, perfect, and complete (Merriam-Webster Dictionary). Excellency of knowledge is that wisdom giveth life to them that have it. *(Eccl. 7:12. For wisdom is a defence, and money is a defence: but the excellency of knowledge is, that wisdom giveth life to them that have it.).*

Let us consider the biblical explanations for wisdom. 'Wisdom' means to fear God *(Prov 1:7 -The fear of the LORD is the beginning of knowledge: but fools despise wisdom and instruction)* and 'to fear God' means to depart from evil.

Prov.3:7- Be not wise in thine own eyes: fear the LORD, and depart from evil; Prov 8:13-The fear of the LORD is to hate evil: pride, and arrogancy, and the evil way, and the froward mouth, do I hate; Job 28:28- And unto man he said, Behold, the fear of the Lord, that is wisdom; and to depart from evil is understanding). The knowledge of the holy (one) [i.e. consciousness of God] is understanding *(Prov.9:10 - The fear of the LORD is the beginning of wisdom: and the knowledge of the holy is understanding).* Anyone that walks in uprightness fears the Lord *(Prov. 14:2) He that walketh in his uprightness feareth the LORD: but he that is perverse in his ways despiseth him).* A wise man hates what God hates *(Prov.6:16-19).* These six things doth the LORD hate: yea, seven are an abomination unto him:

Prov 6:17 A proud look, a lying tongue, and hands that shed innocent blood, Prov 6:18 An heart that deviseth wicked imaginations, feet that be swift in running to mischief,

Prov 6:19 A false witness that speaketh lies, and he that soweth discord among brethren. Anyone that does not seek after God lacks understanding *(Rom 3:11 There is none that understandeth, there is none that seeketh after God).*

Body tissues/organs flourish with activity but suffer atrophies with disuse, and damages with misuse. Please exercise and use your brain!

Part II

Doctrine Of Divine Wisdom And Knowledge

ivine wisdom or wisdom of God is wisdom that originates wholly from God and it is of God. It is quite distinct from man's wisdom or the wisdom of the world. It is rooted and established in the fear of God, love of God and holiness.

What is Divine Wisdom?

The wisdom of God is a mystery to men and it is hidden from men of this world. Men of the world have never been able to understand the wisdom of God in the design and creation of the universe, its structure and organisation, sustainability and conservation of the universe and its overall purpose and goal (**Eccl.3:11**; **Eccl.8:17**). Since the creation of the universe, the mystery of the wisdom of God cannot and will never be unravelled by wisdom of men. It was ordained by God for saints to seek and understand the hidden and mysterious wisdom of God for their glory (**1Cor. 2:7**; **Prov. 23:2**; **Deut. 29:29**). We also know that the mind or heart of our eternal and immortal king is unsearchable and cannot be comprehended with the wisdom of the world (**Prov.23:3**) or the wisdom of the princes of the world of this world but only by those that have the mind of God.

There are at least 8(eight) notable characteristics of divine wisdom which are always exhibited by the possessors of divine wisdom and knowledge. (***Jas 3: 17***- *But the wisdom that is from above is first pure, then peaceable, gentle, and easy to be entreated, full of mercy and good fruits, without partiality, and without hypocrisy)*

DIVINE WISDOM IS: (JAS 3:17).

(1) Pure – chaste, holy and clean without sin or evil intentions.

(2) Peaceable (***Heb 12:14*** *Follow peace with all men, and holiness, without which no man shall* see *the Lord).* Divine wisdom ensures peaceful co-existence always.

(3) Gentle – meek, humble, modest and kind. Divine wisdom is not provocative but easy-going.

(4) Easily entreated – not stubborn. Divine wisdom is not stubborn but easily convinced to see the best reasoning.

(5) Full of mercy (v.17) – always forgiving and performing acts of mercy to all men without bitterness or hardness of heart.

(6) Full of good fruits. Divine knowledge and wisdom is always associated with the fruit of the Holy pirit.

Gal. 5:22-. But the fruit of the Spirit is love, joy, peace, longsuffering, gentleness, goodness, faith, **Gal 5:23-** *Meekness, temperance: against such there is no law.*

(7) Without partiality – Divine wisdom is not discriminatory (i.e. having no respect for persons). *Jas 2:9 -But if ye have respect to persons, ye commit sin, and are convinced of the law as transgressors.*

(8) Without hypocrisy – Divine wisdom is open, honest, genuine, sincere and true (v. 17). Also wisdom speaks of herself as being true in *Prov 8:7 -For my mouth shall speak truth; and wickedness is an abomination to my lips.* **Prov 8:8** *-All the words of my mouth are in righteousness; there is nothing froward or perverse in them).*

Divine wisdom speaks righteousness and truth without crookedness or evil. It does not lead to sorrow because the gift or blessing of God does not lead to sorrow. These attributes can be compared with the characteristics of false or worldly wisdom.

Earthly Wisdom

Wisdom of men or earthly wisdom refers to the excellency of speech, eloquent oration and the higher reasoning of men. This wisdom includes the debate, logic, ideologies and philosophies of men that are entirely human, natural and earthly and has nothing to do with the wisdom and power of God. This was the reason Saint Paul asserted that faith in God should not be built on the wisdom of men but in the power of God. (**1Cor. 2:5**-*That your faith should not stand in the wisdom of men, but in the power of God).*

The wisdom of this world profiteth nothing and will come to nought. The wisdom of this world comprises (i) the wisdom of the ordinary or average men and (ii) the wisdom of the prince of the world. The wisdom of prince of the world comprises the wisdom of earthly nobles and that of the spiritual authorities in higher places. The world has witnessed many theories and hypoteses in all fields of human endeavours which were accepted globally but with time these assertions were proven to be wrong, thereby coming to nought. (**1Cor 2:6**).

I Cor 2:6 -Howbeit we speak wisdom among them that are perfect: yet not the wisdom of this world, nor of the princes of this world, that come to nought,

This is wisdom that its origin is of the earth and has no relation with God. It is devilish and sensual. God has pronounced a curse unto men that pride themselves in early wisdom (**Isa. 5:21**) with a destruction. We know that earthly knowledge puffs up a man (**I Cor. 8:1**; **Isa**. **29:13-14**). Earthly wisdom (**Jas. 3:14-16**) also has these characteristics (i) bitter envying and (ii) strife. Bitter envying may be understood as acrid or pungent ill-will in the possessor of earthly wisdom. Strife may be understood as fighting that leads to contentious factions.

Jas 3:14-But if ye have bitter envying and strife in your hearts, glory not, *and lie not against the truth. **Jas 3:15**-This wisdom descendeth not from above, but is earthly, sensual, devilish. **Jas 3:16**-For where envying and strife is, there is confusion and every evil work.*

Wherever earthly wisdom is prevalent, there is confusion and manifestation of evil works as earthly wisdom exhibits the works of the flesh *(**Gal.5:19-21**)*.

***Gal 5:19**-Now the works of the flesh are manifest, which are these; Adultery, fornication, uncleanness, lasciviousness, **Gal 5:20** Idolatry, witchcraft, hatred, variance, emulations, wrath, strife, seditions, heresies, **Gal 5:21**-Envyings, murders, drunkenness, revellings, and such like: of the which I tell you before, as I have also told you in time past, that they which do such things shall not inherit the kingdom of God.*

The possessor of worldly wisdom portrays the works of the flesh in his life or daily living. Wise men cannot understand folly and wickedness, so also fools do not understand wisdom *(**Tit 1:15** -Unto the pure all things are pure: but unto them that are defiled and unbelieving is nothing pure; but even their mind and conscience is defiled)*. Only a depraved mind understands depravity and its rationale, based on his wealth of experience in foolishness. The wise man does not understand depravity due to his lack of experience in depravity.

Thus a good man should not challenge or compete with a fool or a sinner in matters of foolishness and wickedness because he does not possess the mindset for wickedness nor years of experience in foolishness. It is not in the habit or character of a righteous man to commit sin *(**1Jn 3:9** -Whosoever is born of God doth not commit sin; for his seed remaineth in him: and he cannot sin, because he is born of God.)*

Who is Divine Wisdom?

Christ Jesus is the true wisdom of God. In the Holy Scriptures, our Lord Jesus Christ is the wisdom of God *(1 Cor. 1:24- But unto them which are called, both Jews and Greeks, Christ the power of God, and the wisdom of God; **Col. 2:3**- In whom are hid all the treasures of wisdom and knowledge)*. He is the embodiment of the wisdom of God. We also see that in God or in the mystery (here implies knowledge of gospel) is hidden all the treasures of wisdom and knowledge *(**Col. 2:9**-For in him dwelleth all the fulness of the Godhead bodily. **Col 2:10**-And ye are complete in him, which is the head of all principality and power)*.

As our Lord Jesus Christ is wisdom, He is also the way and the door to true wisdom with all the treasures of wisdom and knowledge in God the Father. One can safely assert that our triune God himself is the fullness of divine wisdom personified. For anyone to be endowed with divine wisdom and knowledge which is embodied in Christ Jesus, he or she needs to have faith in Christ Jesus and abide in him.

John 14:6 -Jesus saith unto him, I am the way, the truth, and the life: no man cometh unto the Father, but by me.

John 10:9- I am the door: by me if any man enter in, he shall be saved, and shall go in and out, and find pasture.

PLACE (SOURCE) OF DIVINE WISDOM

Job 28:12-14-But where shall wisdom be found? and where is the place of understanding? Job 28:13-Man knoweth not the price thereof; neither is it found in the land of the living. Job 28:14-The depth saith, It is not in me: and the sea saith, It is not with me.

Job had inquired of the place where wisdom and understanding can be found. He pointed out clearly that divine wisdom is not found in the land of the living, in the depth of earth or in the sea.

True wisdom and knowledge is from God who gives without upbraiding (*Jas. 1: 5- If any of you lack wisdom, let him ask of God, that giveth to all men liberally, and upbraideth not; and it shall be given him; Eccl. 2:26- For God giveth to a man that is good in his sight wisdom, and knowledge, and joy: but to the sinner he giveth travail, to gather and to heap up, that he may give to him that is good before God. This also is vanity and vexation of spirit*).

True wisdom is from above (i.e. from God in heaven) *Jas.3:17-But the wisdom that is from above is first pure, then peaceable, gentle, and easy to be intreated, full of mercy and good fruits, without partiality, and without hypocrisy*).

PRICE OF DIVINE WISDOM

The price of wisdom and understanding is above man's comprehension neither can it be valued with all gemstones or pearls as in *Job 28:15 -It cannot be gotten for gold, neither shall silver be weighed for the price thereof. Job 28:16- It cannot be valued with the gold of Ophir, with the precious onyx, or the sapphire. Job 28:17-The gold and the crystal cannot equal it: and the exchange of it shall not be for jewels of fine gold. Job 28:18 -No mention shall be made of coral, or of pearls: for the price of wisdom is above rubies. Job 28:19 -The topaz of Ethiopia shall not equal it, neither shall it be valued with pure gold. Job 28:20-Whence then cometh wisdom? and where is the place of understanding? Job 28:21 -Seeing it is hid from the eyes of all living, and kept close from the fowls of the air. Job 28:22 -Destruction and death say, We have heard the fame thereof with our ears. Job 28:23 -God understandeth the way thereof, and he knoweth the place thereof.*

Job 28:24 -For he looketh to the ends of the earth, and seeth under the whole heaven; Job 28:25 -To make the weight for the winds; and he weigheth the waters by measure. Job 28:26 -When he made a decree for the rain, and a way for the lightning of the thunder:

Job 28:27 -Then did he see it, and declare it; he prepared it, yea, and searched it out. Job 28:28 -And unto man he said, Behold, the fear of the Lord, that is wisdom; and to depart from evil is understanding.

Based on the price, source and definition Of wisdom, we see clearly, that only God knows (custodies) the way or path to wisdom and He alone knows the place of understanding (*Job 28:23*).

Wisdom is hidden from man and its price is not known to man, i.e. it is above man's comprehension (*Job 28:13 Man knoweth not the price thereof; neither is it found in the land of the living*). Similarly, the only other thing described in the scripture as being of immense value and priceless, for which nothing can be given in its exchange is the soul of man. Interestingly too, this is also above the comprehension of man because men do not yet know the value of their souls (**Matt 16:26**; **Mk 8:37**).

The price of wisdom is above rubies. This means that wisdom is priceless and cannot be weighed and valued (**Job 28: 15-19**). Priceless gifts are not given out to everyone on the streets except the person meets the requirements or qualifications for them. In this discourse, God is the source of true wisdom. Excellent wisdom is of God and He gives it to the wise (*Dan. 2:21*; *Eph. 1:17*).

Dan 2:21-And he changeth the times and the seasons: he removeth kings, and setteth up kings: he giveth wisdom unto the wise, and knowledge to them that know understanding:

Eph 1:17-*That the God of our Lord Jesus Christ, the Father of glory, may give unto you the spirit of wisdom and revelation in the knowledge of him:*

How to Acquire Divine Wisdom, Understanding and Knowledge

It is very important to obtain God's wisdom, knowledge and understanding. These are a few ways through which one can acquire these priceless assets:

You can get wisdom by (i) **asking of God in prayers** Every saint is required to ask God for wisdom (*Jas 1:17-Every good gift and every perfect gift is from above, and cometh down from the Father of lights, with whom is no variableness, neither shadow of turning*) just as Solomon asked and received, even with more blessings. (*II Chro.1:10-12. Give me now wisdom and knowledge, that I may go out and come in before this people: for who can judge this thy people, that is so great? II Ch 1:11 And God said to Solomon, Because* *this was in thine heart, and thou hast not asked riches, wealth, or honour, nor the life of thine enemies, neither yet hast asked long life; but hast asked wisdom and knowledge for thyself, that thou mayest judge my people, over whom I have made thee king: **2Ch 1:12** Wisdom and knowledge is granted unto thee; and I will give thee riches, and wealth, and honour, such as none of the kings have had that have been before thee, neither shall there any after thee have the like.*

***1Kings 4:29**-And God gave Solomon wisdom and understanding exceeding much, and largeness of heart, even as the sand that is on the sea shore. **1Ki 4:30**-And Solomon's wisdom excelled the wisdom of all the children of the east country, and all the wisdom of Egypt.*

Ask in faith from God, the giver of wisdom *(**Jas. 1: 5-6**).*

***Jas1:5** - If any of you lack wisdom, let him ask of God, that giveth to all men liberally, and upbraideth not; and it shall be given him). **Jas 1:6**-But let him ask in faith, nothing wavering. For he that wavereth is like a wave of the sea driven with the wind and tossed).*

(ii) **Desiring and seeking wisdom and knowledge** (*Matt. 7:7-8*). *Matt 7:7*-Ask, and it shall be given you; seek, and ye shall find; knock, and it shall be opened unto you: *Matt 7:8*-For every one that asketh receiveth; and he that seeketh findeth; and to him that knocketh it shall be opened. One should desire and seek for wisdom and knowledge of God with all his heart, with all his soul and with all his might. (***Prov.2:3-7**- Yea, if thou criest after knowledge, and liftest up thy voice for understanding; **Prov 2:4**- If thou seekest her as silver, and searchest for her as for hid treasures; **Prov 2:5** -Then shalt thou understand the fear of the LORD, and find the knowledge of God. **Prov 2:6** For the LORD giveth wisdom: out of his mouth cometh knowledge and understanding. **Prov 2:7** He layeth up sound wisdom for the righteous: he is a buckler to them that walk uprightly).*

(iii) Knowing God: his attributes and his ways. By devoting time, energy and resources to study and know the being and attributes of God through the Holy Scriptures because knowledge of the Holy is understanding (**Prov. 9:10b**). Few of these divine attributes are his holiness, glory, power, majesty, righteousness, wisdom, perfection, providence, riches, sovereignty, authority, immanence, dominion, judgment, love, immutability, immortality, infallibility, transcendence, greatness, self- sufficiency, inexhaustibility, grace, mercy, faithfulness, omniscience, omnipotence, omnipresence, patience, fatherly disposition, fore-knowledge, goodness, infinite nature, eternity, trinity and self-existence. You can only find God (who is the fullness of wisdom and knowledge) when you seek for Him diligently and earnestly with all your heart, with all your soul and with all your might (***Deut. 4:29**- But if from thence thou shalt seek the Lord thy God, thou shall find him, if thou seek him with all thy heart and with all thy soul*).

(iv) Regeneration (new birth) - At new birth, the Spirit of God regenerates and quickens the spirit of man and the spirit of wisdom starts functioning in the believer. The Spirit of God brings knowledge and wisdom, and uncreated life of God into the being of the new believer. The knowledge of God renews in us a new man after the image of God as we accept our Lord Jesus Christ as our Saviour *(**Col 3:10**- And have put on the new man which is renewed in knowledge after the image of him that created him).*

(v) Having a child-like disposition in life. It is one having the innocence of a child with simple faith and ever willing and ready to learn. The revelation of the mysteries of God is very accessible to the saints especially those that are humble *(**Matt 11:25**-At that time Jesus answered and said, I thank thee, O Father, Lord of heaven and earth, because thou hast hid these things from the wise and prudent, and hast revealed them unto **babes.; Lk 10:21, Mk 4:11**-And he said unto them, Unto you it is given to know the mystery of the kingdom of God: but unto them that are without, all these things are done in parables).* These scripture portions show that knowledge and wisdom are available to those that have come to Christ Jesus as little children (unassuming and not critical but receptive) and dwelling in him. Every saint needs to develop and sustain a child-like disposition, being gentle and meek, in order to receive from God.

(vi) Studying and doing the commandments of God (Deut.4:6) *"Keep therefore and do them; for this is your wisdom and your understanding in the sight of the nations, which shall hear all these statutes, and say, Surely this great nation is a wise and understanding people".*

Love God with all your being and keep his commandments. Read hard and be knowledgeable in other endeavors of life. God lays up sound wisdom for the righteous **(Prov. 2:7)**. Practice makes perfect. As one begins the business of wisdom in small measures, God adds increase and perfects him in his pursuit of wisdom or any other virtue.

The word of God is able to make one wise unto salvation through faith in Christ Jesus **(II Tim 3:15)** and also makes a man of God perfect in all things and furnishes him unto all good works **(II Tim 3:17)**. The word of God contains divine rules and wisdom to govern and perfect man in Christ Jesus.

(vii) The baptism of the Holy Spirit:

When saints are baptized by the Holy Spirit, they are automatically endued with the fullness of Godhead which includes the wisdom, understanding and knowledge of God. This baptism imparts the life and virtue of God on saints in measures as God wills **(Prov.1:23; 17:27; I Cor. 12:11; I Jn 2: 20,27)**.

Prov 1:23-Turn you at my reproof: behold, I will pour out my spirit unto you, I will make known my words unto you.

Prov 17:27-He that hath knowledge spareth his words: and a man of understanding is of an excellent spirit.

I Jn 2:20-But ye have an unction from the Holy One, and ye know all things. I Jn 2:27- But the anointing which ye have received of him abideth in you, and ye need not that any man teach you: but as the same anointing teacheth you of all things, and is truth, and is no lie, and even as it hath taught you, ye shall abide in him.

(viii) Earnestly seek for it in righteousness and holiness.

Matt. 6:33-But seek ye first the kingdom of God, and his righteousness; and all these things shall be added unto you).

We must seek first the coming and the realization of the kingdom of God and its righteousness then we will receive the wisdom of God. Every saint seeking for divine wisdom and knowledge gets involved in prayers and actualization of the kingdom of God on earth through evangelism or soul-winning strategies. Expansion of the kingdom of God in the hearts of men will cause knowledge, wisdom and glory of God to abound, manifest and cover the whole earth. Sometimes in one's life, one may desire and seek for something good from God with wrong motives which we are conscious of or with some deep-seated evil motive which one may not be very conscious of it. With such wrong motives, it is impossible to obtain anything from God (*Eccl.2:26 For God giveth to a man that is good in his sight wisdom, and knowledge, and joy: but to the sinner he giveth travail, to gather and to heap up, that he may give to him good before God. This also is vanity and vexation of spirit*). Divine understanding is also guaranteed for those that seek the Lord (*Prov.28:5 Evil men understand not judgment: but they that seek the LORD understand all things.*).

(ix) **Wisdom can be acquired as a gift of the Holy Spirit.** The Holy Spirit endues the saints with word of wisdom and word of knowledge being gifts of the Holy Spirit for the service and work of God (*1Cor 12:8- For to one is given by the Spirit the word of wisdom; to another the word of knowledge by the same Spirit*). The inspiration of the Almighty giveth men understanding (*Job 32:8 -But there is a spirit in man: and the inspiration of the Almighty giveth them understanding*).

The Spirit of God in the saint enlightens him, being the greatest teacher and counselor, that is the reason one must look unto the Most High for perfection and guidance (*1Jn 2:20- But ye have an unction from the Holy One, and ye know all things, 1Jn 2:27 But the anointing which ye have received of him abideth in you, and ye need not that any man teach you: but as the same anointing teacheth you of all things, and is truth, and is no lie, and even as it hath taught you, ye shall abide in him*)

God wants every saint to increase in wisdom and knowledge (*Col 1:9 For this cause we also, since the day we heard it, do not cease to pray for you, and to desire that ye might be filled with the knowledge of his will in all wisdom and spiritual understanding*).

A Christian must be led by the Spirit of God in order to have divine wisdom, be rational and discerning as a spiritual man. The spiritual man examines {questions}, and judges all things (*I Cor. 2:15-16. But he that is spiritual judgeth all things, yet he himself is judged of no man. 1Co 2:16 -For who hath known the mind of the Lord, that he may instruct him? But we have the mind of Christ).* Foolish men are blind to spiritual things {things of God} *1Cor.1:18). For the preaching of the cross is to them that perish foolishness; but unto us which are saved it is the power of God).*

(x) Saints interceding unto God on behalf of other believers for the spirit of wisdom, revelation and understanding. Saint Paul desired and prayed for saints to be filled with wisdom and spiritual understanding. *Col.1:9- For this cause we also, since the day we heard it, do not cease to pray for you, and to desire that ye might be filled with the knowledge of his will in all wisdom and spiritual understanding; **Eph. 1:16-17-** Cease not to give thanks for you, making mention of you in my prayers; That the God of our Lord Jesus Christ, the Father of glory, may give unto you the spirit of wisdom and revelation in the knowledge of him*

Similarly, saints should intercede with God on behalf of other saints for the granting of divine wisdom and knowledge. Pastors, parents, mentors and teachers should intercede on behalf of their children for the bestowal of divine wisdom and knowledge.

(xi) **Subjection to trials and sufferings**

Sometimes, God may graciously subject saints to trials, wants, persecutions and sufferings of life to gain wisdom through experience. One may have to suffer loss, affliction and sacrifice all to attain the excellency of the knowledge of Christ Jesus *(Phil.3:8. Yea doubtless, and I count all things but loss for the excellency of the knowledge of Christ Jesus my Lord: for whom I have suffered the loss of all things, and do count them but dung, that I may win Christ).* Sorrow, suffering or sadness helps to make man better (wiser) at heart *(Eccl 7:3. Sorrow is better than laughter: for by the sadness of the countenance the heart is made better)*

Spiritual walk is an unfolding experience in God with time. The longer one is in the presence of God, the more spiritual experience he acquires and the more God increases his wisdom and knowledge (**II Cor 3:18**). Thus, with the ancient is wisdom, and in length of days is understanding *(Job 12:12) With the ancient is wisdom; and in length of days understanding ; Job 32:7 I said, Days should speak, and multitude of years should teach wisdom).* God commands us to honour ancient in the Lord as they are they are the custodians of divine wisdom and knowledge (especially experiential spiritual knowledge) consequent of their long years of sojourn on earth.

(Lev 19:32) Thou shalt rise up before the hoary head, and honour the face of the old man, and fear thy God: I am the LORD.

(xii) Vibrant Spirit-filled Companionship: When one associates with vibrant wise and experienced spirit- filled persons, this relationship energizes him to be wise and to do great exploits. He that walketh with wise men shall be wise (**Prov. 13:20**-He that walketh with wise *men* shall be wise: but a companion of fools shall be destroyed). It is a known fact that iron sharpeneth iron, so keeping company with wise men makes one wise (**Prov. 27:17**- *Iron sharpeneth iron; so a man sharpeneth the countenance of his friend*).

(xiii) Adherence to Godly Instructions and Counsel: These godly instructions and counsels may be in form of divine revelations in the scriptures, by the gifts of the Holy Spirit and by counsel by saints of God. **Mat 7:24** -*Therefore whosoever heareth these sayings of mine, and doeth them, I will liken him unto a wise man, which built his house upon a rock:* Saints that heed godly instructions and counsel make progress in life and become wise (**Prov. 19:20**-*Hear counsel, and receive instruction, that thou mayest be wise in thy latter end*; **Prov.28:7a**-*Whoso keepeth the law is a wise son*). Men are blessed of God because they do not heed the instruction or the counsel of the wicked not minding how good it may seem. (**Ps 1:1a**- Blessed *is* the man that walketh not in the counsel of the ungodly).

(xiv) Emptying oneself of earthly wisdom: One has to be broken and emptied oneself of all forms of earthly wisdom (including misconception, false doctrines, heresies and knowledge of occultism) in order to be filled by divine wisdom and knowledge. One has to become a fool, so that he may be wise (**1Cor. 3:18**-*Let no man deceive himself. If any man among you seemeth to be wise in this world, let him become a fool, that he may be wise*). One cannot know and understand God by his own earthly wisdom or the wisdom of the world (**1Cor 1:19-21** -*For it is written, I will destroy the wisdom of the wise, and will bring to nothing the understanding of the prudent. Where is the wise? where is the scribe? where is the disputer of this* *world? hath not God made foolish the wisdom of this world? For after that in the wisdom of God the world by wisdom knew not God, it pleased God by the foolishness of preaching to save them that believe).*

(xv) Studying and silently meditating on the Scriptures: Apart from daily reading of the Bible especially as one uses yearly Bible reading plan, one has to embark on personal study and meditation on the scriptures in silence **(ll Tim. 3:15-17; Deut. 4:6)**. It will help saints greatly if they read good and sound biblical literature that will enhance their spiritual growth not erroneous letters that killeth the soul and the spirit. Furthermore, having Pastors with divine knowledge and wisdom to feed saints is an added advantage **(Jer. 3:5)**.

One must read the whole (entire) word of God and know his entitlements, rights, responsibilities and necessities for spiritual growth and warfare (*Prov.2:6- For the LORD giveth wisdom: out of his mouth cometh knowledge and understanding*). This knowledge of the scripture will help every saint to know God, not to err in our hearts *(**Mat 22:29**-Jesus answered and said unto them, Ye do err, not knowing the scriptures, nor the power of God.; **Heb. 3:10** - Wherefore I was grieved with that generation, and said, They do alway err in their heart; and they have not known my ways.; **Ps. 95:10**. Forty years long was I grieved with this generation, and said, It is a people that do err in their heart, and they have not known my ways).*

(xvi) Fearing or reverencing God in all ways of life: By understanding the fear of God and reverencing Him with awe in all our dealings in life, with all our heart, with all our soul and all our might, do we find wisdom and knowledge of God (***Prov. 2:5**- Then shalt thou understand the fear of the LORD, and find the knowledge of God;*

Job 28:28- *And unto man he said, Behold, the fear of the Lord, that is wisdom; and to depart from evil is understanding; **Prov. 8:13; Prov. 9:10**)*

(xvii) Developing the mind of Christ: Saints are beseeched to develop the mind of our Lord Jesus Christ who is the fullness of Godhead and the embodiment of all wisdom and knowledge of God **(Phil 2:5)**.

***Phil 2:5**-Let this mind be in you, which was also in Christ Jesus:*
In order to develop the mind of Christ that custodies the wisdom and

knowledge of God, there are certain pre-requisites that are needed to be fulfilled just like our Lord Jesus Christ did. A saint must (Phil. 2:2-8)

— Possess divine love (I **Cor.13; Phil.2:2**)
— Have one mind and one accord with true saints (**Phil.2:2**)
— Have lowliness of mind (**Phil.2:3**)
— Not do anything through strife or vain glory (**Phil.2:3**)
— Esteem others better than himself (**Phil.2:3**)
— Consider his own things and also the things of others (**Phil.2:4**)
— Not be or seek to be equal with God (**Phil. 2:6**)
— Make himself of no reputation (**Phil.2:7**)
— Take upon himself the form of a servant (**Phil.2:7**)
— Humble himself (**Phil.2:8**)
— Be obedient unto death, even the death of the cross (**Phil.2:8**)

Finally, R.A. Torrey in *What the Bible Teaches,* suggested these modified steps to acquire wisdom *(James 1: 5 –7):*

1. Admit your lack of wisdom of God
2. Will (set your mind) to do the will of God
3. Ask definitely for divine wisdom, knowledge, understanding and guidance without doubt.
4. Confidently accept divine wisdom.
5. Continuously set your heart to know God and increase in the wisdom and knowledge of God.

Apply wisdom and revelation daily, step by step as one lives on earth. As one makes good use of the wisdom and knowledge of God, just like any other talent or gift, he is increased, established and perfected in them. Wisdom of God is gotten through faith in Christ Jesus and God the father. Knowledge of God increases when a saints continually fellowships or communes with God. (**1Cor 3:18**) On the contrary, knowledge of God is depreciated or decreased and corrupted when one communes with the evil ones (**1Cor.15:34**).

WHEN TO GET DIVINE WISDOM

Every child is born with foolishness, childishness (bad aspects) or sin. A child can easily learn about God. Early childhood stage is the right moment to get or increase in the wisdom and knowledge of God. It is a known fact that foolishness is bound in the heart of a child, but the rod of correction shall drive it far from him (*Ps. 51:5. Behold, I was sharpen in iniquity; and in sin did my mother conceive me*).

Naturally, men prefer darkness and foolishness because we were shaped in iniquity and in sin were we conceived (*Jn. 3: 19b- and men loved darkness rather than light, because their deeds were evil*). We must seek wisdom and knowledge early in our youth (*Prov. 8:17- I love them that love me; and those that seek me early shall find me.*). It is always highly rewarding to seek God early even now as new born babes in Christ Jesus (*Is. 26: 9- With my soul have I desired thee in the night; yea, with my spirit within me will I seek thee early: for when thy judgments are in the earth, the inhabitants of the world will learn righteousness*).

God wants every saint to teach and ensure that their offspring acquire divine wisdom and knowledge (**Gen 18:9**). It is extremely important for teachers and parents to teach knowledge and understanding of doctrines early in life to their children *Is. 28: 9. Whom shall he teach knowledge? and whom shall he make to understand doctrine? them that are weaned from the milk, and drawn from the breasts*). Seek God's wisdom immediately one comes to the realization of these priceless assets at any stage of one's life while one's talents are fresh, vibrant and his memory is strong. If one does not seek God early daily or hearken unto him, one shall reap the fruit of his evil way and be destroyed by the prosperity of fools (*Prov.1:29-32*):

Prov 1:29- For that they hated knowledge, and did not choose the fear of the LORD: Prov 1:30-They would none of my counsel: they despised all my reproof. Prov 1:31-Therefore shall they eat of the fruit of their own way, and be filled with their own devices. Prov 1:32-For the turning away of the simple shall slay them, and the prosperity of fools shall destroy them.

Every saint must bring up their children with virtues and nobility unto perfection in body, soul and spirit. Children with wisdom and of noble upbringing and training are always sought after (*Dan. 1:4-Children in whom was no blemish, but well favoured, and skillful in all wisdom, and cunning in knowledge, and understanding science, and such as had ability in them to stand in the king's palace, and whom they might teach the learning and the tongue of the Chaldeans).*

Spiritual men should exhibit virtues especially wisdom, knowledge, faith and love far above those of their generation. Spiritual men should have foresight with clear and deeper understanding of the scriptures, concerning the future and the perfect will of God because they possess the Spirit of God. This heart rending lamentation of God should not apply to any saint:

For my people are foolish, they have not known me; they are sottish children, and they have none understanding: they are wise to do evil, but to do good they have no knowledge. (Jer 4:22)

*The man who comes to a right belief about God is relieved of ten thousand problems- **A. W. Tozer** (Knowledge of the Holy)*

Part III

Necessity Of Divine Wisdom And Knowledge

emonstration of the wisdom of God in the affairs of life brings joy and blessing to men that possess the wisdom of God and also to men that hear the wisdom and benefit from it (**I King 10: 8**) and reverence to God (**I Kings 3: 28**). King Solomon displayed creative wisdom in his organisation of his kingdom, architecture and building construction, proverbs, business ventures, army and chariots, navy and ships, apparel, royal court arrangement and proceedings, food, throne, woodwork and carvings of brass, silver and gold, (**1King 10:1- 22**) that he exceeded all the kings of the earth for riches and for wisdom (**I King 10:23).**

Necessity of Divine Wisdom and Knowledge

(Col. 1:9-11) For this cause we also, since the day we heard it, do not cease to pray for you, and to desire that ye might be filled with the knowledge of his will in all wisdom and spiritual understanding; Col 1:10 That ye might walk worthy of the Lord unto all pleasing, being fruitful in every good work, and increasing in the knowledge of God; Col 1:11 Strengthened with all might, according to his glorious power, unto all patience and longsuffering with joyfulness;

Considering the Bible passage above, divine knowledge gives glorious power, makes us fruitful on every good work, and perfects our characters. We need to know the truth, which is the fullness and embodiment of divine wisdom and knowledge, so that the truth can set us free **(Jn. 8:32, 36).** By knowing our Lord Jesus Christ, his being and his attributes in the scriptures as the truth, divine wisdom and knowledge, and fullness of God liberates saints from bondage.

The knowledge of God increases faith and drives away unbelief/fear/doubt. With knowledge, we can demand for rendition of account of stewardship by our leaders and resist any manipulation or usurpation of our rights and entitlements by whatever means the evil ones may use.

Evil leaders (in church and society) in order to control, and manipulate their followers and defraud them of their resources, do everything to ensure that their followers are poor, ignorant and foolish regarding their status, rights and entitlements. They also ill-inform or misinform them concerning their blessings and benefits. They distort facts of life and misrepresent the truth.

These leaders (symbolized as wolves in the word of God) seduce the people, take away the key of knowledge from the people and hinder them from entering into the fullness of joy. *(Luke 11:52. Woe unto you, lawyers! for ye have taken away the key of knowledge: ye entered not in yourselves, and them that were entering in ye hindered).*

Hypocritical leaders pretend to worship God in spirit, feigning close relationship with God, but take away the true knowledge of God by nullifying it and substituting with customs and traditions of men (**Matt. 15: 7-9**). *Mat 15:7-Ye hypocrites, well did Esaias prophesy of you, saying, **Mat 15:8**-This people draweth nigh unto me with their mouth, and honoureth me with their lips; but their heart is far from me. **Mat 15:9**-But in vain they do worship me, teaching for doctrines the commandments of men.*

They do not accept knowledge of God and they also prevent others from accepting it. By this, the people are denied entry into the kingdom of God and unto the good life of God *(Matt. 23:13-15-Woe unto you, scribes and Pharisees, hypocrites! for ye compass sea and land to make one proselyte, and when he is made, ye make him twofold more the child of hell than yourselves).* They use all kinds of false doctrines and means to seduce and control people including the saints, who are deficient of the wisdom and knowledge of God.

All these point to the fact that lack of knowledge destroys people *(Hos. 4:6 - My people are destroyed for lack of knowledge: because thou hast rejected knowledge, I will also reject thee, that thou shalt be no priest to me: seeing thou hast forgotten the law of thy God, I will also forget thy children).* Also, where there is no vision from the prophets, teachers, and leaders(judges) in divine will and men of divine knowledge and wisdom to counsel, the people perish *(Prov. 11: 14 - Where no counsel is, the people fall: but in the multitude of counsellors there is safety).* Saints in the positions of leadership are to create and instill the perfect vision of life and of God for men to aspire to and be guided.

We need the fullness of wisdom and knowledge of God to live meaningfully in this world of deceit and wickedness. The evil leaders do everything to ensure that their followers lack vision, knowledge and wisdom of God, thus keeping them in perpetual darkness and blindness of heart. (*Eph 4:18-Having the understanding darkened, being alienated from the life of God through the ignorance that is in them, because of the blindness of their heart).* Christians should possess the excellent wisdom of God like Daniel *(Dan. 5: 11).*

Dan 5:11-*There is a man in thy kingdom, in whom is the spirit of the holy gods; and in the days of thy father, light and understanding and wisdom, like the wisdom of the gods, was found in him; whom the king Nebuchadnezzar thy father, the king, I say, thy father, made master of the magicians, astrologers, Chaldeans, and soothsayers;*

Also, divine wisdom and knowledge ensures that the just is delivered from evil, the snares of the enemy and bondage *(Prov.11:9b - but through knowledge shall the just be delivered.).*

Divine knowledge enhances (i) self-discovery: awareness or knowing whom one is: his nature, traits, preferences, desires, aspiration, weaknesses, strengths i.e. self- knowledge (**Prov 14:8a**- *the wisdom of the prudent is to understand his way;* **II Cor. 13:5**- *Examine yourselves, whether ye be in the faith; prove your own selves. Know ye not your own selves, how that Jesus Christ is in you, except ye be reprobates?).* (ii) Self-realization – knowing one's potentials, self-worth, entitlements and endowments like the prodigal son (**Lk 15:11-32**). (iii) Self–actualization i.e. coming to the fullness of life and maximizing one's potentials and opportunities in life.

In addition, if every saint is wise and knowledgeable in God, he will:

(1) Overcome bondage and influence of Satan, sin and world in his life. *(**Rev 12:11**-And they overcame him by the blood of the Lamb, and by the word of their testimony; and they loved not their lives unto the death).*

(2) Perfect his salvation in Christ Jesus **Col 3:10**. *And have put on the new man, which is renewed in knowledge after the image of him that created him).* He *will* be made perfect in every virtue in Christ Jesus with the Holy Spirit by constant renewal in the knowledge of God.

(3) Easily discern false prophesies and prophets, false teachings and teachers, misinterpretation and misrepresentation of the word of God. **Eph 4: 15-16**. *That we henceforth be no more children, tossed to and fro, and carried about with every wind of doctrine, by the sleight of men, and cunning craftiness, whereby they lie in wait to deceive* (**II Pet 2**; **Jude 4-19**; **1John 4:1-3**).

(4) Overcome weakness, sicknesses and the workings of evil spirits by our Lord Jesus Christ (*Acts 10:38. How God anointed Jesus of Nazareth with the Holy Ghost and with power: who went about doing good, and healing all that were oppressed of the devil; for God was with him*).

(5) Know the perfect will of God concerning all aspects of his life (*Eph. 5: 17- Wherefore be ye not unwise, but understanding what the will of the Lord is.; Ps.25:14-The secret of the LORD is with them that fear him; and he will shew them his covenant*).

(6) Understand spiritual gifts and their manifestations

(7) Easily identify the wiles of the devil in our society (*Rom.16:17- Now I beseech you, brethren, mark them which cause divisions and offences contrary to the doctrine which ye have learned; and avoid them.*

Rom 16:18-For they that are such serve not our Lord Jesus Christ, but their own belly; and by good words and fair speeches deceive the hearts of the simple).

(8) Avoid sin, foolishness and its consequences (*Prov.5:22- His own iniquities shall take the wicked himself, and he shall be holden with the cords of his sins*).

(9) Understand the deceitfulness of the heart of a natural man (**Jer.17: 9**), deceitfulness of sin (**Heb.3: 13**) as well as the deceitfulness of riches (**Matt. 13:22; Mk. 4:19**) and profitability of godliness (**I Tim. 4:8**).

(10) Not be easily deceived and defrauded by Satan even when Satan appears as the angel of light and his agents appear as ministers of righteousness (**II Cor 11:14-15**).

(11) Lay claims or appropriate all his entitlements, rights and blessings (inheritance in Christ Jesus) in this life and in life to come.

(12) Withstand the devil, destroy the works of the devil, and not be slaves to elemental spirits, greedy leaders, hypocrites and mediocre (*I Jn. 3:8- He that committeth sin is of the devil; for the devil sinneth from the beginning. For this purpose the Son of God was manifested, that he might destroy the works of the devil*).

(13) Not make much mistakes or losses regarding management of time, energy, resources and other issues of life

(14) Manifest God's glory in his life through creativity and innovations.

(15) Wage war and destroy the works of the devil and his agents by the command of God and withstand works of darkness without fear of evil (*Judg 3:2 Only that the generations of the children of Israel might know, to teach them war, at the least such as before knew nothing thereof*). We ought to know that we are the instrument of war and vessels of God through which God manifests His glory, power, wisdom and knowledge just like Moses, Elijah, David, and Paul

(16) Build good homes and raise godly families and children unto God. (*Prov.24:3-4-Through wisdom is an house builded; and by understanding it is established: And by knowledge shall the chambers be filled with all precious and pleasant riches*).

(17) Govern the people and rule the society in wisdom at any position or level of authority and be exalted in righteousness

(18) Overcome all wants (*Ps. 23:1; Ps. 34:9. O fear the LORD, ye his saints: for there is no want to them that fear him*).

(19) Unleash his full human potentials and attain well-developed (growth) mindsets.

(20) Exercise and exhibit his faith with works (actions).

(21) Live a well-balanced and fruitful life with the help of the Spirit of God.

(22) Seek redress and justice without fear just like the widow (**Lk. 18:1-8**) that appealed to unrighteous judge

(23) Exhibit and exercise the fruit and gifts of the Spirit in wisdom within divine will.

(24) Expose the works of darkness; because our inability to withstand and /or resist the Devil and expose the works of darkness makes us accomplices of evil.

So many acclaimed affluent persons enrich themselves at the expense of fools, because of their ignorance of the word of God, their ignorance to their entitlements and rights and in addition to their willingness to be exploited and subjugated. These oppressors reap what they did not sow and where they did not sow, even in church where saints do not wage war against evil.

Therefore, in every place a child of God finds him, he should endeavour to know and understand the system, the way it works, the constitution, rules and regulations of the place or organization. Man should not allow himself to be used, manipulated and abused. People must exhibit the wisdom of God. Knowledge of the truth gives a man's will absolute freedom (sovereignty of will). It liberates the will and the mind of man. It is known that where the Spirit of God is, there is liberty; therefore, anyone having the Spirit of God should be in liberty and should also ensure liberty in his ambience (**II Cor.3:17**).

Divine wisdom and knowledge will enhance the awareness of Christians to the fact that the ultimate power in the universe is at their beck and call, they would have changed their circumstances and environments through prayers of faith and good works, thus causing the will of God to be done on earth and his kingdom established on earth speedily.

Permanency of Divine Wisdom

When God blesses a saint with divine wisdom, like every spiritual gift, it stays with him permanently *(Eccl. 2:9. So I was great, and increased more than all that were before me in Jerusalem: also my wisdom remained with me; Rom. 11:29. For the gifts and calling of God are without repentance)* except one becomes an apostate or a reprobate, then the Spirit of God leaves him *(I Sam. 16:14. But the Spirit of the LORD departed from Saul, and an evil spirit from the LORD troubled him).*

Wisdom and understanding can also be regained after its loss *(Daniel 4:34. And at the end of the days, I Nebuchadnezzar lifted up mine eyes unto heaven, and mine understanding returned unto me, and I blessed the most High, and I praised and honoured him that liveth for ever, whose dominion is an everlasting dominion, and his kingdom is from generation to generation).* The Holy Scriptures in its entirety acknowledges the need for divine wisdom and commands us to get wisdom and understanding (**Prov. 4:7**).

(Pro 4:7) Wisdom is the principal thing; therefore get wisdom: and with all thy getting get understanding.

Thinking is the real business of life. Creative Thinkers rule the world – **Venice Bloodworth**

Physical, spiritual and mental gifts and talents must be exercised constantly for effectiveness and growth.

𝔓art IV

𝔅lessings Of 𝔇ivine 𝔚isdom 𝔄nd 𝔎nowledge

Divine wisdom and knowledge

1) Enables man to make profit and be fruitful in his being and his endeavours of life. With favour of God man is guided on how to save and invest in ventures that will lead to his properity (**Isa 48:17** *Thus saith the LORD, thy Redeemer, the Holy One of Israel; I am the LORD thy God which teacheth thee to profit, which leadeth thee by the way that thou shouldest go).*

2) Gives joy and boldness because when one knows God and his fullness, one is full of joy and has no fear *(**Prov. 3:13**-Happy is the man that findeth wisdom, and the man that getteth understanding).*

3) Is a defense and also gives life *(**Prov.8:35.** For whoso findeth me findeth life, and shall obtain favour of the LORD; **Prov 9:11**-For by me thy days shall be multiplied, and the years of thy life shall be increased; **Eccl. 7 :12**-For wisdom is a defence, and money is a defence: but the excellency of knowledge is, that wisdom giveth life to them that have it).*

4) gives divine health that prevents and overcomes all ills and sicknesses *(**Prov 3: 8** It shall be health to thy navel, and marrow to thy bones).*

5) Strengthens, gives inheritance of glory and dispels instability and threats of any kind to the saint *(**Is 33:6.** And wisdom and knowledge shall be the stability of thy times, and strength of salvation: the fear of the LORD is his treasure; **Prov.3:35.** The wise shall inherit glory: but shame shall be the promotion of fools; **Prov. 4:9** - She shall give to thine head an ornament of grace: a crown of glory shall she deliver to thee).*

6) Delivers out of troubles and preserves through divine counsels and strategic planning *(**Prov. 11: 8-9.** The righteous is delivered out of*

trouble, and the wicked cometh in his stead. **Prov 11:9**-*A hypocrite with his mouth destroyeth his neighbour: but through knowledge shall the just be delivered;* **Prov 24:6**-*For by wise counsel thou shalt make thy war: and in multitude of counsellors there is safety.*

7) Gives secured refuge from evil and fear **(Prov.1:33.** *But whoso hearkeneth unto me shall dwell safely, and shall be quiet from fear of evil;* **Ps.112: 1-10**).

8) Surpasses and excels folly **(Eccl.** *2:13-Then I saw that wisdom excelleth folly, as far as light excelleth darkness.).*

9) Gives blessings, length of days, riches, and honour, pleasantness, and peace **(Prov 3:2** *For length of days, and long life, and peace, shall they add to thee;* **Prov. 3:14-18:** **Prov 3:14** *For the merchandise of it is better than the merchandise of silver, and the gain thereof than fine gold.* **Prov 3:15**-*She is more precious than rubies: and all the things thou canst desire are not to be compared unto her.* **Prov 3:16**-*Length of days is in her right hand; and in her left hand riches and honour.* **Prov. 3:17**-*Her ways are ways of pleasantness, and all her paths are peace.* **Prov. 3:18** -*She is a tree of life to them that lay hold upon her: and happy is every one that retaineth her;*

10) Guides man to build a good home by marrying a good wife and raising up godly children **(Prov. 24:3**-*Through wisdom is an house builded; and by understanding it is established:* **Prov 24:4**-*And by knowledge shall the chambers be filled with all precious and pleasant riches).*

11) *Enables* saints to know the perfect will of God in matters of life as a result of their deeper knowledge of God and in-dwelling Spirit of God in them **(Eph 5:17**- *Wherefore be ye not unwise, but understanding what the will of the Lord is;* **Prov 3:32**-*For the froward is abomination to the LORD: but his secret is with the righteous).*

12) Gives material and spiritual riches (without sorrows and regrets), promotion and honour **(Prov.8:18-19.** *Riches and honour are with me; yea, durable riches and righteousness.* **Prov. 8:19**- *my fruit is better than gold, yea, than fine gold; and my revenue than choice silver).*

13) Enhances good leadership and governance **(Prov.8:14-16.** *Counsel is mine, and sound wisdom: I am understanding; I have strength.*

*Prov. 8:15-By me kings reign, and princes decree justice. **Prov.** 8:16-By me princes rule, and nobles, even all the judges of the earth).*

14) Enhances creativity in all walks of life. (***Prov.8:12*** *I wisdom dwell with prudence, and find out knowledge of witty inventions, (**Prov.** 8:22-30)-Prov. 8:22-The LORD possessed me in the beginning of his way, before his works of old. **Prov. 8:23** I was set up from everlasting, from the beginning, or ever the earth was. **Prov. 8:24** When there were no depths, I was brought forth; when there were no fountains abounding with water. **Prov. 8:25**-Before the mountains were settled, before the hills was I brought forth: **Prov.-8:26**-While as yet he had not made the earth, nor the fields, nor the highest part of the dust of the world. **Prov. 8:27**-When he prepared the heavens, I was there: when he set a compass upon the face of the depth:*

*__Prov. 8:28__-When he established the clouds above: when he strengthened the fountains of the deep: **Prov. 8:29**-When he gave to the sea his decree, that the waters should not pass his commandment: when he appointed the foundations of the earth: **Prov. 8:30**-Then I was by him, as one brought up with him: and I was daily his delight).*

Great kings and emperors that ruled the world had the best counselors (wise and knowledgeable men) in their kingdoms and empires in positions of authorities. Examples are:

Pharaoh had Joseph; David had Ahitophel; Nebuchadnezzar and Darius had Daniel; Ahasuerus had counselors. Also consider Alexander the Great, Julius Caesar and other great men of old ruled the world and established their domains through good counselors as strategists and policy makers.

Kings and Kingdoms (e.g. Rehoboam's reign) failed because they had bad counselors (fools) in positions of authorities or as nobles. Obviously, in life, business, politics, religion, etc. many people succeeded or failed due to good or bad counseling they heeded as the case may be. Nations, dynasties or individuals will always either succeed or fail based on the kind of counseling they adhere to. In order to succeed in life, seek and make use of divine counsel in all your endeavours and pursuits. Wisdom is good with an inheritance; and by it there is profit to them that see the sun *Eccl.7:11- Wisdom is good with an inheritance: and by it there is profit to them that see the sun).*

God longs to bless His children who will consecrate and dedicate themselves unto Him and good works so that they can manifest His glory and might on earth wherever they are. Saints are ambassadors of Christ, whose authority they should exercise freely to establish justice, righteousness and godliness in their domains. In their manifestations of God's glory, many people will see the wisdom of God in them and his deliverance for them and turn unto God *(Deut. 4:6- Keep therefore and do them; for this is your wisdom and your understanding in the sight of the nations, which shall hear all these statutes, and say, Surely this great nation is a wise and understanding people; Esther 8:17- And in every province, and in every city, whithersoever the king's commandment and his decree came, the Jews had joy and gladness, a feast and a good day. And many of the people of the land became Jews; for the fear of the Jews fell upon them).*

All through the ages, worshippers of God were always blessed physically, materially, mentally, spiritually, militarily and politically. They were blessed in every facet of life because God was with them **(Gen. 39:2-6; Deut. 28: 1-14)**.

Gen 39:2-And the LORD was with Joseph, and he was a prosperous man; and he was in the house of his master the Egyptian.

Gen 39:3-And his master saw that the LORD was with him, and that the LORD made all that he did to prosper in his hand.

Gen 39:4-And Joseph found grace in his sight, and he served him: and he made him overseer over his house, and all that he had he put into his hand.

Gen 39:5-And it came to pass from the time that he had made him overseer in his house, and over all that he had, that the LORD blessed the Egyptian's house for Joseph's sake; and the blessing of the LORD was upon all that he had in the house, and in the field.

Gen 39:6-And he left all that he had in Joseph's hand; and he knew not ought he had, save the bread which he did eat. And Joseph was a goodly person, and well favoured

Command on Divine Wisdom and Knowledge

Every saint is instructed to get wisdom and get understandimg. He is also expected to be filled with wisdom and be increased in wisdom as our Lord Jesus Christ did (*Lk. 2:40- And the child grew, and waxed strong in spirit, filled with wisdom: and the grace of God was upon him, Lk 2:52- And Jesus increased in wisdom and stature, and in favour with God and man ; Prov. 4:5 Get wisdom, get understanding: forget it not; neither decline from the words of my mouth; Prov 4:7-Wisdom is the principal thing; therefore get wisdom: and with all thy getting get understanding*).

Every saint is also required to ask God of His wisdom (*Jas. 1:5 If any of you lack wisdom, let him ask of God, that giveth to all men liberally, and upbraideth not; and it shall be given him ; Prov. 2:6-7 -For the LORD giveth wisdom: out of his mouth cometh knowledge and understanding. Prov. 2:7-He layeth up sound wisdom for the righteous: he is a buckler to them that walk uprightly.*

On getting the wisdom of God, one should not corrupt it with sin or unrighteousness like some apostates in the Bible or even as the Devil did (**Eze. 28:17**) or fail to make good use of it as the wicked, slothful and unprofitable servant did (**Matt:25:24-30**). It is always God's earnest desire that his children are filled with the knowledge of His will in all wisdom and spiritual understanding (*Col. 1: 9. For this cause we also, since the day we heard it, do not cease to pray for you, and to desire that ye might be filled with the knowledge of his will in all wisdom and spiritual understanding*).

Every saint is also commanded to fear God and keep his commandments which is wisdom (*Eccl. 12:13. Let us hear the conclusion of the whole matter: Fear God, and keep his commandments: for this is the whole duty of man;* **Ps. 111:10-** *The fear of the LORD is the beginning of wisdom: a good understanding have all they that do his commandments: his praise endureth for ever).* Anyone that has the wisdom of God fears God and keeps his commandments. Also anyone that has divine wisdom, loves God with all his heart, with all his soul and with his might and keeps God's commandments *(**Deut. 6:5-** And thou shalt love the LORD thy God with all thine heart, and with all thy soul, and with all thy might; **Deut. 4:6-**Keep therefore and do them; for this is your wisdom and your understanding in the sight of the nations, which shall hear all these statutes, and say, Surely this great nation is a wise and understanding people;*

Exhibition of nature and gestures of divine love abounds more in saints with increased wisdom and knowledge of God *(**Phil.1:9** -And this I pray, that your love may abound yet more and more in knowledge and in all judgment).* Always pray and strive for more divine wisdom and knowledge.

Duties of Teachers, Parents, Coaches and Leaders

ruly, training up (teaching, mentoring or parenting) a person (physically, spiritually, socially, professionally and mentally) sincerely with love, takes away much virtue from the trainers and teachers. The teachers (parents) lay up or sacrifice for the benefits of others (**2 Cor. 12:14**-*Behold, the third time I am ready to come to you; and I will not be burdensome to you: for I seek not yours, but you: for the children ought not to lay up for the parents, but the parents for the children*).

Nevertheless, these parents and teachers have to ensure the command of God (**Gen. 18:19.** *For I know him, that he will command his children and his household after him, and they shall keep the way of the LORD, to do justice and judgment; that the LORD may bring upon Abraham that which he hath spoken of him ;* **Deut. 6:6-7** *And these words, which I command thee this day, shall be in thine heart:*

Deut 6:7-*And thou shalt teach them diligently unto thy children, and shalt talk of them when thou sittest in thine house, and when thou walkest by the way, and when thou liest down, and when thou risest up*).

God commands also that parents should receive appropriate honour and reward for their effort in child upbringing and training (**Deut. 5:16.** *Honour thy father and thy mother, as the LORD thy God hath commanded thee; that thy days may be prolonged, and that it may go well with thee, in the land which the LORD thy God giveth thee :* **Eph. 6:1.** *Children, obey your parents in the Lord: for this is right*).

God has also commanded that teachers and other labourers in the vineyard of God should be partakers of provisions in the temple of God and should be catered for and appreciated for their efforts in training and perfecting the young and older saints (**I Cor. 9:13-14** - *Do ye not know that they which minister about holy things live of the things of the temple? and they which wait at the altar are partakers with the altar? 1Cor 9:14-Even so hath the Lord ordained that they which preach the gospel should live of the gospel.* ; **Gal. 6:6** - *Let him that is taught in the word communicate unto him that teacheth in all good things; I Tim. 5:18-For the scripture saith, Thou shalt not muzzle the ox that treadeth out the corn. And, The labourer is worthy of his reward*).

Teachers are custodians of knowledge. Leaders, parents and teachers should be filled with the spirit of wisdom and knowledge. They should be deeply rooted and established in wisdom and knowledge and also ensure that their knowledge is true, updated, and be continually transformed by the renewing of the mind. The duty of a teacher and a leader is to teach people knowledge and understanding The duty of a teacher and a leader is to teach people knowledge and understanding and emancipate the people (**Prov. 1: 1-5; Eccl. 12:9-10.** *And moreover, because the preacher was wise, he still taught the people knowledge; yea, he gave good heed, and sought out, and set in order many proverbs. **Eccl. 12:10-**The preacher sought to find out acceptable words: and that which was written was upright, even words of truth; **Jer.3:15.** And I will give you pastors according to mine heart, which shall feed you with knowledge and understanding*) (**Lk. 4:18-19.** *The Spirit of the Lord is upon me, because he hath anointed me to preach the gospel to the poor; he hath sent me to heal the broken hearted, to preach deliverance to the captives, and recovering of sight to the blind, to set at liberty them that are bruised, **Lk. 4:19-**To preach the acceptable year of the Lord*).

The teacher or leader should teach people and caused them to understand the scriptures (**Neh. 8:8** -*So they read in the book in the law of God distinctly, and gave the sense, and caused them to understand the reading*) and also help the young ones to fully embrace the gospel and enjoy the benefits and blessings therein such as power over death, sin, sickness, fear and the devil.

Heb. 2:14-15. *Forasmuch then as the children are partakers of flesh and blood, he also himself likewise took part of the same; that through death he might destroy him that had the power of death, that is, the devil; **Heb 2:15** And deliver them who through fear of death were all their lifetime subject to bondage*). The teacher's duty is to enlighten Christ's followers to see light out of obscurity and darkness (**Acts. 26:18.** *To open their eyes, and to turn them from darkness to light, and from the* *power of Satan unto God, that they may receive forgiveness of sins, and inheritance among them which are sanctified by faith that is in me.*

The teacher is to guide the children (physical and spiritual children), with the guidance and help of the Holy Spirit, on the right paths to follow to the glorious light of God: **Isa 42:16** -*And I will bring the blind by a way that they knew not; I will lead them in paths that they have not known: I will make darkness light before them, and crooked things straight. These things will I do unto them, and not forsake them.* The work of the teacher is directed and enhanced by the greatest teacher and counselor, the Holy Spirit who also enhances good memory (**Jn.6:45**- *It is written in the prophets, And they shall be all taught of God ; But the Comforter, which is the Holy Ghost, whom the Father will send in my name, he shall teach you all things, and bring all things to your remembrance, whatsoever I have said unto you* ; **I Jn. 2: 27**- *But the anointing which ye have received of him abideth in you, and ye need not that any man teach you: but as the same anointing teacheth you of all things, and is truth, and is no lie, and even as it hath taught you, ye shall abide in him*).

Godly training in holiness and knowledge of God is to uplift man from childishness, and to maturity in or fullness of God (that is having the mind of God and the Spirit of God).

It is the duty of teachers (leaders) to make the word of God real to the young ones by making them hear, see, have faith on, and touch the word of life (*I **Jn. 1:1-2**. That which was from the beginning, which we have heard, which we have seen with our eyes, which we have looked upon, and our hands have handled, of the Word of life;* **1Jn 1:2** *(For the life was manifested, and we have seen it, and bear witness, and shew unto you that eternal life, which was with the Father, and was manifested unto us*) and also perfect (equip) the children unto every good works **II Ti 2:21** *If a man therefore purge himself from these, he shall be a vessel unto honour, sanctified, and meet for the master's use, and prepared unto every good work ;* **Heb. 13:21**-*Make you perfect in every good work to do his will, working in you that which is well pleasing in his sight, through Jesus Christ; to whom be glory for ever and ever, Amen;* **II Tim. 3:17**-*That the man of God may be perfect, thoroughly furnished unto all good works;* **Heb. 10:24**. *And let us consider one another to provoke unto love and to good works*).

Teachers should endeavour to do God's work faithfully and whole-heartedly in order to be blessed and be rewarded appropriately by God (***Heb. 10:35*** -*Cast not away therefore your confidence, which hath great recompence of reward*). If a teacher or leader does God's work deceitfully a curse is upon him (*Jer. 48:10a-Cursed be he that doeth the work of the LORD deceitfully*). God enjoins every teacher to teach himself and also live by example (*Rom.2:21-Thou therefore which teachest another, teachest thou not thyself? thou that preachest a man should not steal, dost thou steal?*).

If I may ask you on behalf of our children: "Teacher, carest thou not that we perish?" (*Mk. 4:38. And he was in the hinder part of the ship, asleep on a pillow: and they awake him, and say unto him, Master, carest thou not that we perish?*). Parents, pastors and teachers should wake up from their slumber and teach and care for the children lest they perish.

In your course of duty as a teacher, do your best, but if any man wishes to be ignorant let him be ignorant (*1Cor. 14:38. But if any man be ignorant, let him be ignorant*).

Teachers are required to expose the works of darkness and also cast down imaginations, false teachimgs and every high thing (seen and unseen) that exalts itself against the knowledge of God (*II Cor.10:5. Casting down imaginations, and every high thing that exalteth itself against the knowledge of God, and bringing into captivity every thought to the obedience of Christ*). Teachers should teach the whole of the scriptures (**Jn. 15:15; Acts.20:27**) because the extent of their students' progress depends on the depth of the visions created in them and the extent of divine knowledge, love and truth instilled in them.

Saints should pray unto God to give messengers, leaders and teachers who are after God's heart to feed the people with knowledge and understanding (*Eccl. 12:9; Jer. 3:15*). Teachers should be very patient with their students while teaching a lesson because scriptural truths are imbibed at different rates by different persons. It took Nebuchadnezzar seven years to learn a lesson on the sovereignty of God (**Dan. 4**) and took Prophet Jonah quite some time to learn a lesson on divine ownership (**Jonah 4**). They should not be companions to foolish men but are to depart from their presence (**Prov 14:7**- *Go from the presence of a foolish man, when thou perceivest not in him the lips of knowledge*).

Now the end of the commandment is charity out of a pure heart, and of a good conscience, and of faith unfeigned: (1Ti 1:5)

Do not invest your resources in vanities or foolishness; neither should you invest in fools or vile persons. A fool though living in foolishness seeks the blessing of the wise.

Part V

Foolishness And Wickedness

𝔍 t may deepen our understanding of the excellency of wisdom and knowledge and the dire need to teach or to get wisdom and knowledge, if we consider the term **'fool'** and its definition and explanation. The knowledge on the character of a fool will help us to easily identify a fool by his fruits and avoid him.

CHARACTERISTICS OF A FOOL

A fool is a person who lacks understanding and wisdom and despises wisdom and instructions *(Prov. 1:7- The fear of the LORD is the beginning of knowledge: but fools despise wisdom and instruction);* How often do we see foolish men reject good and wise counsel by saying that it is their lives, they have every right and they are free to live it the way they choose without being bothered?

Fools make a mockery of sin *(Prov. 14:9- Fools make a mock at sin: but among the righteous there is favour).* They laugh at or make fun of sin as being unimportant and it is of no effect on them. By mocking at sin, they are saying, in effect what can sin possibly do to them?

Fools take sin as sport *(Prov. 10: 23- It is as sport to a fool to do mischief: but a man of understanding hath wisdom).* They view sin as good fun or an interesting game.

Fools hate knowledge *(Prov. 1:22- How long, ye simple ones, will ye love simplicity? and the scorners delight in their scorning, and fools hate knowledge?).* A common characteristic of a fool is hatred for knowledge. This hatred for knowledge is seen in their hatred for God, who is God of knowledge, wise men and wise counsels. This hatred may be veiled (or covert) or may be overt. In the covert example, the fool may pretend with joy and appreciation that he likes knowledge, loves God of knowledge and wise men but inwardly hating knowledge and the custodians of knowledge. In the overt example, the fool openly declares that he hates knowledge, hates God and wise counsels through his actions and words. He also declares that he does not want to hear of or have any dealing with knowledge.

A fool is a senseless person (lacking the faculty of perceiving by means of sense organs); witless (lacking intelligence, reasoning power or understanding), silly (stupid), foolish (unwise), simple person who lacks wisdom, understanding and discretion. A fool is a wicked, impious (profane) and vile (morally despicable and repulsive) person (Dake's Bible). A fool is a wicked reprobate, destitute of morality and godliness.

A fool is a person that says in his heart there is no God (**Ps. 14:1a-** *The fool hath said in his heart, There is no God*). He may not publicly declare that there is no God because of fear of men, but his words, actions and thoughts always point to the fact that he does not in any way reverence God in his life. Neither does he believe that God exists and he is worthy of His worship, honour and glory. As a fool lacks wisdom and knowledge of God, he lacks the Spirit of God (Holy Spirit) who is the Spirit of knowledge and wisdom (**Is. 11:2, 9-** *And the spirit of the LORD shall rest upon him, the spirit of wisdom and understanding, the spirit of counsel and might, the spirit of knowledge and of the fear of the LORD*).

We should consider more attributes of a fool. He:

- Lives as if God does not exist and does no good. A fool says or does whatever he wants without honour, respect or fear of God even if he preaches the Bible daily. He does not care about the existence of God (**Ps.53:1-***The fool hath said in his heart, There is no God. Corrupt are they, and have done abominable iniquity: there is none that doeth good*).
- Hides hatred with lying lips (**Prov.10:18-***He that hideth hatred with lying lips, and he that uttereth a slander, is a fool*).
- Utters slander and deceit. (**Prov.10:18**); speaks froward things, lies and deceit (**Prov.14:8-***The wisdom of the prudent is to understand his way: but the folly of fools is deceit*). The key point of folly or foolishness of fools is a life of lies and hypocrisy and the utterance of lies, deceit and slander.
- Despises instructions, counsel and corrections from his superiors and inferiors (**Prov.15:5-***A fool despiseth his father's instruction: but he that regardeth reproof is prudent*).
- Trusts in his own heart {self} (**Prov.28:26** - *He that trusteth in his own heart is a fool: but whoso walketh wisely, he shall be delivered*).
- Practices hypocrisy and causes mischief (**Prov.4:16** - *For they sleep not, except they have done mischief; and their sleep is taken away, unless they cause some to fall*).

- Does not believe the revelation of God (*Luke 24:25 - Then he said unto them, O fools, and slow of heart to believe all that the prophets have spoken:*)
- Is filled with the wisdom of the world and depends on his own wisdom, which is foolishness unto God (*I Cor. 1:20*). *Where is the wise? where is the scribe? where is the disputer of this world? hath not God made foolish the wisdom of this world? the*
- Does not reason intelligibly
- Practices wickedness daily as his food and drink (*Prov. 4:17-For they eat the bread of wickedness, and drink the wine of violence*)
- Entangles himself to death with an adulterous woman because he does not heed instructions (*Prov.5:8-13- Remove thy way far from her, and come not nigh the door of her house: Prov 5:9- Lest thou give thine honour unto others, and thy years unto the cruel: Prov 5:10 Lest strangers be filled with thy wealth; and thy labours be in the house of a stranger; Prov 5:11-And thou mourn at the last, when thy flesh and thy body are consumed. Prov 5:12- And say, How have I hated instruction, and my heart despised reproof; Prov 5:13-And have not obeyed the voice of my teachers, nor inclined mine ear to them that instructed me!*).
- Graduates from shame to shame as he continues in foolishness and receives beating with the rod in the process (*Prov.3:35-The wise shall inherit glory: but shame shall be the promotion of fools*
- Destroys his own soul and even his household in his cruelty by his words and actions (*Prov.6:32-But whoso committeth adultery with a woman lacketh understanding: he that doeth it destroyeth his own soul ; Prov. 11:17-The merciful man doeth good to his own soul: but he that is cruel troubleth his own flesh*);
- Dies for want {or destitution} of wisdom (*Prov.10:21-The lips of the righteous feed many: but fools die for want of wisdom*).
- Despises and destroys his neighbour for one reason or so. His reason may be religious, racial, physical, emotional, social, cultural, intellectual or so. This supposed tenable reason may be based on a bias, prejudice, envy, hatred, jealousy, anger, and inferiority or superiority complex (*Prov.11:9-An hypocrite with his mouth destroyeth his neighbour: but through knowledge shall the*

*just be delivered. **Prov 11:12**-He that is void of wisdom despiseth his neighbour: but a man of understanding holdeth his peace).*

- Meddles in strife that does not concern him and causes it to escalate instead of seeking peace or peaceful resolution *(**Prov.20:3**-It is an honour for a man to cease from strife: but every fool will be meddling).*

- Is a servant to the wise of heart (***Prov.11:29***-He that troubleth his own house shall inherit the wind: and the fool shall be servant to the wise of heart).

- Is perverse in all his ways (***Prov.19:3***-The foolishness of man perverteth his way: and his heart fretteth against the LORD).

- Departs not from evil or foolishness (***Prov.13:19***-The desire accomplished is sweet to the soul: but it is abomination to fools to depart from evil; **Prov. 27:22**-Though thou shouldest bray a fool in a mortar among wheat with a pestle, yet will not his foolishness depart from him).

- Is known by a multitude of words (Eccl.5:3-For a dream cometh through the multitude of business; and a fool's voice is known by multitude of words);

- Proclaims and exhibits his foolishness openly in the society by his words, reasoning and actions (***Prov.12:23***-A prudent man concealeth knowledge: but the heart of fools proclaimeth foolishness; **Prov 13:16**- Every prudent man dealeth with knowledge: but a fool layeth open his folly)

- Follows after vain persons and vain pursuits; and indulges in vanities and insanities. *(**Prov.12:11**) He that tilleth his land shall be satisfied with bread: but he that followeth vain persons is void of understanding);*

- Does not pay his vows to God and to man. He does not keep his words, thus he lacks integrity (***Eccl.5:4***. When thou vowest a vow unto God, defer not to pay it; for he hath no pleasure in fools: pay that which thou hast vowed);

- Rages confidently in evil. This means that he reiterates his correctness, rights and reasons in his misdeeds and evil words while over-stepping bounds (***Prov.14:16***-A wise man feareth, and departeth from evil: but the fool rageth, and is confident).

- Rejoices in folly (***Prov.15:21***-Folly is joy to him that is destitute of wisdom: but a man of understanding walketh uprightly); Fools are just like little children, who in their ignorance, happily play with harmful devices or substances that can kill them because they do not know. Also, they happily take deadly risks or stunts for the fun of it without considering the resultant effects, implications or consequences.

- Has no delight in wisdom and understanding (*Prov.18:2-A fool hath no delight in understanding, but that his heart may discover itself*).
- Drinks alcohol (*Prov.20:1-Wine is a mocker, strong drink is raging: and whosoever is deceived thereby is not wise*);
- Utters all {folly of} his mind (*Prov.29:1-A fool uttereth all his mind: but a wise man keepeth it in till afterwards*)

Emphatically, a fool is a wicked person *(Is. 26:10)* who:

I.   Will not learn righteousness{ways of God} even when favour is shown to him,
II. Deals unjustly with people, and
III. Does not behold the majesty of the Lord

Fools are ever learning, and never able to come to the knowledge of truth *(II Tim. 3:7-Ever learning, and never able to come to the knowledge of the truth).* Therefore, saints of the Most High must walk circumspectly, not as fools, but as wise for our Lord God has no pleasure in fools *(Eph.5:15-See then that ye walk circumspectly, not as fools, but as wise; Rom 8:8 So then they that are in the flesh cannot please God).*

Men exhibit foolishness at different ages and stages of their lives. Some men never seem to outgrow certain levels of foolishness even when they are older and eventually die. Every child is born with foolishness but the rod of discipline drives it away from him.

Consequences of lack of Divine Knowledge

The Bible is replete with examples of men that suffered from the consequences of lack of wisdom and knowledge. Some of the consequences of foolishness are: death, rejection by God, dethronement, the forgetting of our children by God, shame, punishment, dissatisfaction, in-satiation, no increase, loss of mind(i.e. madness), curse, corruption of seed, debasement with contempt, profaning and corrupting priestly covenant, etc. (**Deut. 28:16-68**; **Hos 4:6-11**; **Mal. 2:1-12**). Foolishness or wickedness has several grave consequences. It is an extremely risky and fatal business to be wicked in the society. When the society becomes aware and reacts, the consequences of wickedness affect the fools, their children and their children's children, except they learn wisdom by accepting Christ Jesus who is divine wisdom and knowledge personified (*Ex. 20:5-6. Thou shalt not bow down thyself to them, nor serve them: for I the LORD thy God am a jealous God, visiting the iniquity of the fathers upon the children unto the third and fourth generation of them that hate me; Exo 20:6- And shewing mercy unto thousands of them that love me, and keep my commandments(Deut. 5:9).* It is a known fact that the secret of the Lord is with the righteous *(Prov. 3:32 -For the froward is abomination to the LORD: but his secret is with the righteous ; Ps. 25:14-The secret of the LORD is with them that fear him; and he will shew them his covenant)* whereas the curse of the Lord is in the house of the wicked *(Prov. 3:33-The curse of the LORD is in the house of the wicked: but he blesseth the habitation of the just).*

It is a very precarious life to be wicked and foolish because of the losses one stands to incur when one is judged by God or when one is discovered by men. These losses include loss of assets and investment, risk to one's life and well-being, wastage, loss of good reputation and relationship in the society and punishment by the law

A fool is doomed for a fall (*Prov. 10:8-10-The wise in heart will receive commandments: but a prating fool shall fall; Prov 10:9-He that walketh uprightly walketh surely: but he that perverteth his ways shall be known; Prov 10:10-He that winketh with the eye causeth sorrow: but a prating fool shall fall).* Always, he/she walks headlong into calamities. Fools, because of their transgressions and because of their iniquities, are afflicted *(Ps. 107:17 Fools because of their transgression, and because of their iniquities, are afflicted).* This shows that so many problems, sickness, and afflictions of men would have been averted if only men were wise and godly. A sinner or a fool destroys much good *(Eccl. 9:18. Wisdom is better than weapons of war: but one sinner destroyeth much good).* God deals or relates with us according to our sin or folly and according to our level of divine wisdom and knowledge *(Job 42:8b - and my servant Job shall pray for you: for him will I accept: lest I deal with you after your folly, in that ye have not spoken of me the thing which is right, like my servant Job).*

When fools or charlatans fill up positions of authorities in government, society, church, organizations and families, such entities are doomed. *(Eccl. 10: 5-7: There is an evil which I have seen under the sun, as an error which proceedeth from the ruler: Eccl 10:6-Folly is set in great dignity, and the rich sit in low place. Eccl. 10:7-I have seen servants upon horses, and princes walking as servants upon the earth, also. Eccl. 10:16-17: Woe to thee, O land, when thy king is a child, and thy princes eat in the morning! Eccl 10:17-Blessed art thou, O land, when thy king is the son of nobles, and thy princes eat in due season, for strength, and not for drunkenness!)*

God abhors all wastage *(Matt 15:37-And they did all eat, and were filled: and they took up of the broken meat that was left seven baskets full).* When time, energy and resources are entrusted into the hands of fools to manage, you cannot imagine the resultant colossal waste *(Eccl 9:18b).*

A wicked person in leadership controls every aspect of the system using all kinds of evil machinations and principles and does not encourage any innovations or development that will liberate the system or make it big in order not to lose control. He is scared of wisdom and knowledge, advancement and enlightenment. He may even initiate its decimation or disintegration into miniature sizes which can easily be controlled by him and micromanage by his stooges. The laws that are enacted are detrimental to growth and development in such corporations,

This is why we are not making much progress in some of our cultures and organizations. Knowledgeable and wise persons should strive for leadership and executive positions, fill up positions of authorities and responsibilities, enforce righteousness and ensure rectitude and continence. It is a known fact that righteousness exalts and uplifts the nation but corruption and sin are a reproach to a nation.

There are so many manifestations of foolishness namely:

- Death
- Calamities *(Ps. 40:12. For innumerable evils have compassed me about: mine iniquities have taken hold upon me, so that I am not able to look up; they are more than the hairs of mine head: therefore my heart faileth me)*;
- Sicknesses and decadence {rottenness, corruption}*(Ps. 38:5-My wounds stink and are corrupt because of my foolishness)*.
- Inability to understand signs of times in the society as predicted by our Lord Jesus Christ.
- Inability to understand one's destiny as a wise man;
- losses;
- Inability to do good or tackle appropriately key issues of life: health, shelter, well-being, food, clothing; education, and self-actualization.
- Despondency: lack of seriousness in one's well- being and lack of interest in one's life and development.
- Dissipation: Wasting one's life, talent, time, energy and resources in unprofitable ventures and pursuits (vanities).

in or foolishness separates us from God and subjects us to curses, madness, blindness and confusion of heart / mind *(Deut. 28:28-29-The LORD shall smite thee with madness, and blindness, and astonishment of heart: And thou shalt grope at noonday, as the blind gropeth in darkness, and thou shalt not prosper in thy ways: and thou shalt be only oppressed and spoiled evermore, and no man shall save thee).*

Sin renders us naked, vulnerable, and brings shame to us *(Ex. 32:25-And when Moses saw that the people were naked; (for Aaron had made them naked unto their shame among their enemies); Gen.3:7- And the eyes of them both were opened, and they knew that they were naked; and they sewed fig leaves together, and made themselves aprons).*

Lack of wisdom and knowledge deprives us of the blessings of the gospel *(Acts 26:18- To open their eyes, and to turn them from darkness to light, and from the power of Satan unto God, that they may receive forgiveness of sins, and inheritance among them which are sanctified by faith that is in me;* If we are ignorant of the teachings or doctrines of Christ Jesus, crafty men (charlatans and hypocrites) will deceive us into all forms of false doctrines thereby exploiting us and limiting our increase and growth in God *(Col 2:18 Let no man beguile you of your reward in a voluntary humility and worshipping of angels, intruding into those things which he hath not seen, vainly puffed up by his fleshly mind,*

Col 2:19-And not holding the Head, from which all the body by joints and bands having nourishment ministered, and knit together, increaseth with the increase of God). If we allow false teachers and prophets to lead us, we suffer with them the same consequences and punishments *(Ezek. 14:9-10: And if the prophet be deceived when he hath spoken a thing, I the LORD have deceived that prophet, and I will stretch out my hand upon him, and will destroy him from the midst of my people Israel. Eze 14:10-And they shall bear the punishment of their iniquity: the punishment of the prophet shall be even as the punishment of him that seeketh unto him ;(II Jn.1:10-11). 2Jn 1:10-If there come any unto you, and bring not this doctrine, receive him not into your house, neither bid him God speed: II Jn 1:11-For he that biddeth him God speed is partaker of his evil deeds).*

Lack of knowledge subjects men to a life of slavery, fear, and bondage (captivity) *(Is.5:1-Therefore my people are gone into captivity, because they have no knowledge: and their honourable men are famished, and their multitude dried up with thirst).* Men are also subjected to poverty, weakness, depravity, subjugation and subservience to the wicked. For instance, if only we know who we are in Christ Jesus and we also know that (i) God (ii) the law (iii) government/society, and (iv) the enforcers of the law are against the wicked or terror, we would have been exerting and taking our rightful positions as 'more than conquerors in Christ Jesus". It is worthy to note that deliverance requires knowledge, wisdom, faith, prayer and fasting and one's personal action towards his well-being.

If we are ignorant of the wiles / devices of the devil, Satan takes advantage of us *(II Cor. 2:11-Lest Satan should get an advantage of us: for we are not ignorant of his devices).* God does not want us to be ignorant about very pertinent issues of life. Many seekers of God are zealous for God without knowledge *(Rom.10:2- For I bear them record that they have a zeal of God, but not according to knowledge).* They undertake spiritual tasks such as fasting, prayers, alms-giving, tithes and works of God without wisdom and knowledge *(Is.58:3-4: Wherefore have we fasted, say they, and thou seest not? wherefore have we afflicted our soul, and thou takest no knowledge? Behold, in the day of your fast ye find pleasure, and exact all your labours. Isa 58:4-Behold, ye fast for strife and debate, and to smite with the fist of wickedness: ye shall not fast as ye do this day, to make your voice to be heard on high).*

Lack of divine wisdom and knowledge deprives saints from receiving any blessings from God *(Jas.4:1-8).* All increase comes from God who is the head of all *(Col 2:19-And not holding the Head, from which all the body by joints and bands having nourishment ministered, and knit together, increaseth with the increase of God).*

*It is foolhardy to seek for life or the living in tombs/graveyards; so also, knowledge, wisdom, love, joy, peace, meaning and essence of life are not found in dead works (**Lk 24:5c** -Why seek ye the living among the dead?)*

Part VI

Knowledge of God

esus Christ said unto his disciples thus "whither I go ye know and the way ye know". But Thomas said unto the Lord "we know not whither thou goest; and how can we know the way? (**Jn. 14:4-5**).

Jn 14:4-And whither I go ye know, and the way ye know. Jn 14:5-Thomas saith unto him, Lord, we know not whither thou goest; and how can we know the way?

It is clear in this discourse of our Lord with the disciples that they did not understand, though taught by the greatest teacher, our Lord Jesus Christ for over two years on several issues of godliness, morality and spirituality. They did not comprehend, understand and know in their consciousness the being of God, the dwelling place of God (that is heaven) and the only way to go to heaven and to be with God which is by salvation through Christ Jesus.

In order to defuse their ignorance of the things of God, our Lord Jesus readily answered him *"I am the way the truth and the life: no man cometh unto the father, but by me".(Jn. 14: 6)* Here once again, our Lord emphasizes the key point of knowing God the Father which is by knowing His only begotten Son, Jesus Christ (**Jn. 17:2-3**). Furthermore, he pointed out to them, a fact that they were not aware of, that since they have seen and beheld our Lord Jesus, it means they know the Father and have seen Him, since God the Father and God the Son are one.

Despite all the explanations of the union or interpenetration of God the Father with God the Son, Philip still expressed more ignorance by saying unto our Lord "Lord show us the father and it sufficeth us" (Jn. 14:8). To this request by Philip, our Lord reiterated the earlier explanation as stated in **Jn 14:9-11**:

Jn 14:9- Jesus saith unto him, Have I been so long time with you, and yet hast thou not known me, Philip? he that hath seen me hath seen the Father; and how sayest thou then, Shew us the Father? Jn 14:10 -Believest thou not that I am in the Father, and the Father in me? the words that I speak unto you I speak not of myself: but the Father that dwelleth in me, he doeth the works. Jn 14:11 -Believe me that I am in the Father, and the Father in me: or else believe me for the very works' sake.

In addition, knowing the being of God the Father, Son and Holy Spirit entitles us to the full baptism of the Holy Spirit which the world cannot receive because they see him not neither do they know him (**Jn. 14:17**).

Jn 14:17-Even the Spirit of truth; whom the world cannot receive, because it seeth him not, neither knoweth him: but ye know him; for he dwelleth with you, and shall be in you.

As earlier stated in a previous subheading of the book on how to acquire divine wisdom, and more discussions on ways of knowing God in a latter subheading, it is also re-emphasized here that in keeping the commandments of God, loving God and having the love of God, a saint will truly and deeply know God because God will manifest Himself to him and make His abode with him (**Jn.14:21,23**).

Jn 14:21- He that hath my commandments, and keepeth them, he it is that loveth me: and he that loveth me shall be loved of my Father, and I will love him, and will manifest myself to him. Jn 14:23-Jesus answered and said unto him, If a man love me, he will keep my words: and my Father will love him, and we will come unto him, and make our abode with him.

Furthermore, knowing God, His word and the revelations of God that have been made accessible and known unto us qualifies or makes us to be true friends of God because servants do not know what their master does but to the saints all things have been made known unto them of the Father (**Jn15:15**). We have access to the whole counsel of God.

Jn 15:15-Henceforth I call you not servants; for the servant knoweth not what his lord doeth: but I have called you friends; for all things that I have heard of my Father I have made known unto you.

Lack of knowledge of God, makes men to hate God, hate and persecute the saints, put them out of the synagogues and kill them thinking they are doing God's service (**Jn 16:2-3**).

Jn 16:2-They shall put you out of the synagogues: yea, the time cometh, that whosoever killeth you will think that he doeth God service. Jn 16:3-And these things will they do unto you, because they have not known the Father, nor me.

The knowledge of God helps saint to behold the glory and majesty of God; his holiness, his righteousness and judgement. One should be filled with the knowledge of God through Bible study, meditation, revelation, fellowship with one another. The knowledge of God helps us to behold the enthronement of our Lord Jesus Christ at the right hand of God with majesty and glory. Our Lord is highly exalted above all (**Phil 2:9-11**).

Phil 2:9*-Wherefore God also hath highly exalted him, and given him a name which is above every name:* ***Phil 2:10****-That at the name of Jesus every knee should bow, of things in heaven, and things in earth, and things under the earth;* ***Phil 2:11****-And that every tongue should confess that Jesus Christ is Lord, to the glory of God the Father.*

Knowing God

We have considered ways of having the wisdom and knowledge of God, which is more or less like having the mindset of God. Also, we have considered ways of acquiring this mindset of God or the wisdom and knowledge of God. Here, we want to look into ways of having the conscious awareness of the being of the most high in our being. God wants man to really know Him deeply: His being, preferences, nature, and attributes, what he loves; what he hates; what gives him pleasure, even extreme pleasure. Unfortunately, man has always been pre-occupied and overwhelmed by the knowledge of fearsome nature of God especially regarding the nakedness and sinfulness of man (Gen. 3:10) and also the bountiful benefits they can derive from God.

Meaning of "To Know"

In Merriam – Webster dictionary "To Know" means

i.   To understand thoroughly; To diligently discern; To have understanding of;
ii. To perceive fully; To acknowledge and declare; To have knowledge of;
iii. To be aware of; To ascertain exactly; To comprehend fully;
iv. To be completely assured or convinced; To make full proof of; Most surely believe in

Therefore, 'To know' God means to have full knowledge and deep awareness in one's consciousness about God: His being, thoughts, will, power, mind, preference, and attributes. This knowledge of God shows that one has studied and loved God closely with keen interest and understood God deeply with all his might, soul (emotions) and spirit (conscience, intellect, will). Such close-up study implies that one has heard of, touched, experienced, tasted of, seen, been with, and communed with God intimately. Divine wisdom and knowledge is exhibited by the possessor of mind of Christ or divine mind (mind of God). Unfortunately, so many saints are like Samuel (**I Sam. 3:1**), who did not yet know God and neither was the word of God revealed to him. Saints must strive to attain the full knowledge of the Son of God (**Eph. 4:13-** *Till we all come in the unity of the faith, and of the knowledge of the Son of God, unto a perfect man, unto the measure of the stature of the fulness of Christ*).

God always desires to have fellowship (communion) with man from the beginning of creation. Mutual fellowship is greatly enhanced when one has good knowledge and understanding of the other. In this constant and continuous fellowship with God, man would have known God intimately and be transformed into His image (**II Cor 3:18**-*But we all, with open face beholding as in a glass the glory of the Lord, are changed into the same image from glory to glory, even as by the Spirit of the Lord*).

Regrettably, man chooses his own way of being as God (**Gen. 3:5**-*For God doth know that in the day ye eat thereof, then your eyes shall be opened, and ye shall be as gods, knowing good and evil*). In spite of this, in order to still achieve His divine ultimate purpose and will of making man a partaker of His divine nature (and image) and be full of knowledge of God, He sent His only begotten Son essentially to reveal God to man, so that he may know him deeply and be conformed to the image of God by the renewing of the mind through wisdom and knowledge of God (**Rom.12:2**-*And be not conformed to this world: but be ye transformed by the renewing of your mind, that ye may prove what is that good, and acceptable, and perfect, will of God*).

It is obvious that one needs to know another intimately in order to have a perfect relationship without hitches (**Amos 3:3**-*Can two walk together, except they be agreed?*). Knowledge of God enhances trust and trust leads to intimate communion. Scarcity of knowledge of God leads to universal corruption (**Rom. 1:28**-*And even as they did not like to retain God in their knowledge, God gave them over to a reprobate mind, to do those things which are not convenient*). We have to be born of God, love God intimately and have close fellowship in order to know God (**1Jn. 4:7**-*Beloved, let us love one another: for love is of God; and every one that loveth is born of God, and knoweth God*).

It is quite evident that the ultimate essence of incarnation of our Lord Jesus Christ was to make manifest the being of God unto man, so that man may know Him. Divine incarnation was actually the climax and culmination of divine manifestations and revelations over the ages. A study of the life and being of our Lord Jesus Christ makes one to know God the Father (***Jn 8:19*** *Then said they unto him, Where is thy Father? Jesus answered, Ye neither know me, nor my Father: if ye had known me, ye should have known my Father also*).

Saints have only emphasized salvation of mankind as the most important aspect of the birth of Jesus Christ. If it were the ultimate goal, there would not have been any need for our Jesus Christ to have taken up human form, be born and lived amongst men, to exemplify and manifest the image and life of God by his being and lifestyle. Through his living amongst men and his being, men were to know God. This is evident when he rebuked his disciples when they requested of our Lord to show them the Father. His rebuke implied that, for all the while he has been with them, his conversations, teachings, healings and performance of miracles, they still do not know him nor his Father who is in heaven **(Matt. 16:13-17; John 14:8-9).**

In his reply, our Lord affirms that it is the heavenly Father that reveals His being unto men. If salvation was the sole purpose, then he would have simply descended on the earth in flesh and be crucified after some days in order to save mankind. It can also be deduced that originally God created man so that by His intimate fellowship with man, he may know him. By this knowledge of God, man will be changed into the same image of God from glory to glory by the Spirit of the Lord (**II Cor. 3:18**-*But we all, with open face beholding as in a glass the glory of the Lord, are changed into the same image from glory to glory, even as by the Spirit of the Lord*).

A scriptural reference that admonishes saints to know God is:

*(**Jeremiah 9:23-24**) Thus saith the LORD, Let not the wise man glory in his wisdom, neither let the mighty man glory in his might, let not the rich man glory in his riches:*

*But let him that glorieth glory in this, that he **understandeth** and **knoweth** me, that I am the LORD which exercise lovingkindness, judgment, and righteousness, in the earth: for in these things I delight, saith the LORD.*

God commands us in his Word to know Him and glory or boast in Him. Unfortunately, man (single or collective) has always boasted or glorified in his royalty/pedigree (genealogy) **I Tim. 1:4;** social status, and learning, **(Phil. 3:5-6)**; gods (idols) **Judges 16:23**; weapons of warfare **(II King 19:10-11)** and in men and princes **(Ps.118:9)**; Men also boast about self-righteousness and piety **(Luke 18:11-12)**; achievement and work **(Dan. 4:30)**. Broadly speaking, there are three major things in which men boast or glory in. They glory in wisdom, might, and riches **(Jer. 9:23)** and God admonishes us emphatically not to glory in all these things.

The only divine condition that man should glory in or boast of is that he should glory in the Lord and that he **understands** and **knows** God (**Jer. 9:24**). These two key words stress the necessity of in-depth knowledge of God: (i) Knowledge of the being of God.

(ii) Knowledge of His attributes and

(iii) Knowledge of what gives him pleasure or delight. This in-depth knowledge of God is basically required in these three phases. The first phase of in-depth knowledge of God or knowing God is to know that I AM THE LORD (GOD). This command is seen severally in the scriptures as God always required of man to **know** Him. The statement " I am the Lord: Ex. 6:7; Jer. 9:24"can be analyzed as follows:

I – The Supreme Being

I am – Self existent and ever living one

The – qualifying superlative

Lord – Jehovah – (Self –existent or Eternal one).

… And ye shall know that I AM THE LORD GOD (**Eze. 37:6, 13**). Here also, the main reason God gives life unto dry bones is that man may know him deeply particularly His being. The whole essence of divine revelation(s), manifestation(s), its reception, its utterance and its performance and fulfillment, is for the people of the earth to know and have this knowledge of the declaration of the most high God that states "I am the LORD GOD" (**Eze. 37:6,13,14; Matt. 27:54**).

The next phase of knowledge of God is to know His attributes: man must know him essentially as the Lord God which exercises loving-kindness, judgment and righteousness in the earth (**Jer. 9:24**). Additionally, though not exhaustive of the attributes of God, man should know God as being kind, faithful, good, longsuffering, forgiving, holy, truthful, etc. This knowledge of the attributes of God helps one to know the things that God takes great pleasure or delight. This is the third phase of the in-depth knowledge of God. For examples, God delights in those who do His will, obey Him absolutely, loves and worships Him in Spirit and in truth.

Knowledge of God includes knowing the being of God, His divine nature, traits and attributes. A saint that knows his God shall be strong and do great exploits (**Dan. 11:32b**-*but the people that do know their God shall* *be strong, and do exploits).* The sole purpose of God performing miracles is for the people of God (**Ex. 6:7**) and unbelievers (**Ex. 7:5**) to know him as the only true God and there is none like him or besides him. (**Ex. 9:14; Ex.10:2; Ps. 135:5**-*For I know that the LORD is great, and that our Lord is above all gods).*

Also, the workings and the exhibition of any of the gifts and fruit of the Holy Spirit is not for the glory of man but for men to know God. All means of divine revelations to man on spiritual aspects and issues of life through dreams, visions, counsels of man, voice of God, visitations of angels, intuition, word of God, prophecies and other means of divine appearances are to increase in man the knowledge of the person and attributes of God and faith in God. If at any instance of divine manifestation or ministration of spiritual gift or working that does not enhance the knowledge of God in man, increase his faith in God or give God all the glory, then it is not of God. In such instance, the practitioner stands accursed and condemned before God (*Acts 12:22*-*And the people gave a shout, saying, It is the voice of a god, and not of a man.*

Act 12:23-*And immediately the angel of the Lord smote him, because he gave not God the glory: and he was eaten of worms, and gave up the ghost)*

God want us to know and understand his attributes. A few of the attributes are;

(i) His glory (**II Cor. 4:6**-*For God, who commanded the light to shine out of darkness, hath shined in our hearts, to give the light of the knowledge of the glory of God in the face of Jesus Christ)*

(ii) His words (scriptures) and his power (**Mk 12:24**-*And Jesus answering said unto them, Do ye not therefore err, because ye know not the scriptures, neither the power of God?)*

(iii) His generous fatherly disposition (**Matt. 7:11**-*If ye then, being evil, know how to give good gifts unto your children, how much more shall your Father which is in heaven give good things to them that ask him?)* ; Lk. 11:13.

(iv) His thoughts and his counsel (**Is 55:8**-*For my thoughts are not your thoughts, neither are your ways my ways, saith the LORD).*

(v) His will (**Col. 1:9; Eph. 1:9**- *Having made known unto us the mystery of his will, according to his good pleasure which he hath purposed in himself*).

In His word, we see that man who knows the being of the Lord God and his attributes always communes with God intimately, exhibits great faith and performs the things that give God great pleasure. Briefly, only few examples will be cited here:

— Our Lord Jesus Christ understands and knows God the Father and totally surrenders to his will which pleased him greatly. God attested to this by saying "this is my beloved son in whom I am well pleased" (**Matt. 3:17**).
— David knew the being of God and His attributes. He also knew that God loves praises, music and worship in his majesty and glory, holiness, righteousness, obedience to His commandments, salvation of his people, and whole-hearted trust and service unto Him. God attested to him that he was a man after his heart (**I Sam 13:14**).
— Abraham knew God and exhibited unwavering faith in God and total obedience unto God by walking before him blameless. And God attested about him that he was a friend of God (**Jas 2:23**)

Ways of knowing God

he ways of acquiring the wisdom and knowledge of God already discussed, are the same ways God use to create awareness in our conscience (consciousness). It is expedient on saints to increase in the knowledge of God by harnessing these divine ways of knowing God. (**Col. 1:10**-*That ye might walk worthy of the Lord unto all pleasing, being fruitful in every good work, and increasing in the knowledge of God*; **II Pet. 3:18**-*But grow in grace, and in the knowledge of our Lord and Saviour Jesus Christ. To him be glory both now and for ever. Amen*).

In order to continuously increase in the knowledge of God, each saint must embark on concerted, conscious, diligent and earnest search for God through Bible study, compliance to revelations of God, absolute obedience to God and to understand the being of God. The knowledge of God comes as an awareness or revelation from Him to our hearts (**Eph. 1:17**). Another way of knowing God is by total obedience to His word as Abraham, David and our Lord Jesus Christ did. Our Lord Jesus Christ performed the will of God whole-heartedly without wavering and because He knew his Father (**Jn. 8:55**).

Evidences of Knowing God

How do we know assuredly that a person knows God? There are some evidences that prove that a saint knows God and abides in him (**I Jn. 2:3-29**); Saint John states clearly that hereby we do know that we know him, if we:

— Wholeheartedly keep the commandments of God (v. 3)
— Keep the word of God and his love is perfected in us (v.5)
— Walk uprightly in perfection as our Lord walked (v. 6)
— Love our brethren and abide in the light of God (v.10)
— Walk not in darkness or exhibit works of darkness (v.11)
— Have clear conscience as our sins are forgiven (v.12)
— Possess deeper knowledge of God as matured spiritual men (v.13)
— Continually exhibit strength in God, and overcome the wicked one (v.13&14)
— Abide richly in the word of God
— Love not the world, neither the things that are in the world (v.15&16).
— Do the will of God (v.17)
— Know the signs of times, (v.18), the manifestations of the antichrist and the move of the Spirit of God.(v.19)
— Remain in unity and fellowship with true children of God (v.19)
— Unction from God to know all thing (v.20)
— Know the truth, which is God (v.21)
— Acknowledge God the father and our Lord Jesus Christ (v.23)
— Abide in Christ and Christ abides in us (24 v-27)

— Have received the promise of eternal life (v. 25)
— Received anointing of God that teaches us all things and redeems us from seduction or seducing doctrines (v.26 &27)
— Practice rightness in our daily living (v.29)

Benefits of Wisdom and Knowledge of God

Through the knowledge of God, saints (**II Pet. 1:1-8**) are

— Recipients of Divine power (v.3)
— Made them beneficiaries of all things that pertain to life and godliness (v.3)
— Living in glory and virtue (v.3)
— Partakers of divine nature (v.4)
— Title holders to exceeding great and precious promises of God (v.4)
— Safe from corruption and lust of the world (v.4) (**II Pet. 2:20**);
— Made fruitful (v.8) in good works of faith.
— Made to grow and abound in faith, virtue, knowledge, temperance, patience, godliness, brotherly kindness and charity (v.5-7)
— Made to be calm in spirit in the face of calamities and adversity (**Ps. 46:10**).
— Refrained from backsliding, forsaking God and worshipping idols (**Eze. 6:7; Eze. 11:10**).
— To do great in presentation of their petitions/prayers before God as in the case of King Hezekiah (**II King 18-19; Is. 37:16-20**)
— Given eternal life (**Jn. 17:3; I Jn. 5:20**)
— Put in check from pride (self-conceit) and be humbled (**Dan 4:17,25-32**)
— Reminded of the being of God, His commandments, judgments and statutes (**Deut. 8:10-18**) in the period of prosperity.

Furthermore, the wisdom and knowledge of God:

— Justifies saints (**Is. 53:11b**-*by his knowledge shall my righteous servant justify many; for he shall bear their iniquities*)
— Gives stability in one's life (**Is. 33:6**-*And wisdom and knowledge shall be the stability of thy times, and strength of salvation: the fear of the LORD is his treasure*).
— Ensures rewards and achievements in life (**Prov. 24:14**-*So shall the knowledge of wisdom be unto thy soul: when thou hast found it, then there shall be a reward, and thy expectation shall not be cut off*).
— Multiplies grace and peace unto the saints (**II Pet. 1:2**- *Grace and peace be multiplied unto you through the knowledge of God, and of Jesus our Lord*)
— Enable saints to be strong and overcome the wicked one (I **John 2:13**-*I write unto you, fathers, because ye have known him that is from the beginning. I write unto you, young men, because ye have overcome the wicked one. I write unto you, little children, because ye have known the Father. 1Jn 2:14- I have written unto you, fathers, because ye have known him that is from the beginning. I have written unto you, young men, because ye are strong, and the word of God abideth in you, and ye have overcome the wicked one*)
— By the knowledge of the Holy, understanding and wisdom, years of life of a man is increased (**Prov. 9:10**-*The fear of the LORD is the beginning of wisdom: and the knowledge of the holy is understanding. Prov 9:11 For by me thy days shall be multiplied, and the years of thy life shall be increased*).

Importance of the knowledge of God

son is just like a slave when he has not grown up to the stage of maturity (mental, spiritual, emotional, social and physical maturity) to be made a crown prince. This is why many saints are in bondage due to lack of knowledge and wisdom of God and insight of life. This illustrates the importance of divine wisdom and knowledge. Some saints with little knowledge may still be in bondage due to their lack of increase in knowledge unto maturity in Christ Jesus that will qualify for or accord them the full status of a crown prince, or joint heir with Christ Jesus.

Saints are commanded to know God (**1Chro. 28:9**) and this knowledge helps in presenting petitions, arguments and prayers before God (**Gen. 18:23-33**). God gives the grace for men to know Him as God with their whole hearts (**Jer. 24:7**-*And I will give them an heart to know me, that I am the LORD: and they shall be my people, and I will be their God: for they shall return unto me with their whole heart*).

Specifically, God may enlarge our knowledge concerning specific attributes of Him. For instance:

i. Knowledge of God concerning His power and holiness really exposes man's hopelessness, helplessness and sinfulness before God (**Ex. 9:28**-*Intreat the LORD (for it is enough) that there be no more mighty thunderings and hail; and I will let you go, and ye shall stay no longer*).

ii. Knowledge of God concerning the divine ownership of the earth keeps man in check concerning covetousness, pride and ungodly search for riches and wealth (**Ex. 9:29**; **Ps. 24:1**-*The earth is the LORD'S, and the fulness thereof; the world, and they that dwell therein*) or harbouring ill-will towards our enemies (**Jon 4**).

iii. Many men of old that had the consciousness or awareness of the sovereignty of God, confessed and worshipped God with all sense of awe and humbleness. Examples are Jethro (**Ex. 18:11**- *Now I know that the LORD is greater than all gods: for in the thing wherein they dealt proudly he was above them*) and Nebuchadnezzar (**Dan.4:1-3, 34-37**).

The knowledge of God is the basis for all blessings of God for this age and for the age to come *(Ps 91:14-Because he hath set his love upon me, therefore will I deliver him: I will set him on high, because he hath known my name)*. Knowing God is a very important topical lesson that should be taught to children especially by guidance of the Spirit of God (**Jer. 31:34**) and great shall be their peace (**Is. 54:13**-*And all thy children shall be taught of the LORD; and great shall be the peace of thy children).*

Saints with the knowledge and wisdom of God are established in righteousness, made far from oppression, fear and terror (**Is. 54:14**). Knowing God liberates men from the bondage of beggarly elements, which by nature are no gods (**Gal. 4:8-9**). Also the knowledge of God unites the saints in faith and perfects them (**Eph. 4:13**-*Till we all come in the unity of the faith, and of the knowledge of the Son of God, unto a perfect man, unto the measure of the stature of the fulness of Christ).*

The word and works of God make believers and men to know and understand God (**Rom. 1:19-20**). The Spirit of God reveals God to men, gives them a heart to know God (**Jer. 24:7**) and teaches saints all things at every stage of life unto maturity in Christ Jesus (**1 Jn.2:20, 27; Heb. 8:10-12**). Earnestly desire and seek knowledge and wisdom of God and thou shall find it.

In all ages, it has always been the earnest desire of saints to know God intimately and deeply after they have had encounter with God. Moses desired wholeheartedly to know God (**Ex. 33:13-23**), whereas Saint Paul desired to know God and His power of resurrection. (**Phil. 3:10**-*That I may know him, and the power of his resurrection, and the fellowship of his sufferings, being made conformable unto his death*). Saint Paul desired wholeheartedly (even with readiness to suffer loss) to know the excellency of the knowledge of Christ Jesus our Lord. He desired to know:

i.   Our Lord Jesus Christ
ii. The power of his resurrection
iii. The fellowship (i.e. sharing in knowledge and experience) of Christ's suffering.

This godly desire and possible attainment would have made Saint Paul to be wholly made conformable to the death and resurrection of our Lord Jesus Christ (**Phil. 3:10-11**).

Saints should earnestly desire and spend considerable time to know God instead of being in a haste to know God. It is also the earnest desire of God (**Hos. 6:6**) more than burnt offering, that his children should ask and receive the knowledge and wisdom of God (**Luke 11:9-13; 1King 3:9-13**). Lack of knowledge of God is always accompanied by the lack of truth and mercy in the land (**Hos. 4:1**) and results in the rejection of the people by God and their subsequent destruction (**Hos. 4:6**). It is this lack of knowledge or revelation of God which pertained to the peace of Jerusalem made Jesus Christ to weep for the city for the destruction that was to come upon it. (**Lk 19:42**-*Saying, If thou hadst known, even thou, at least in this thy day, the things which belong unto thy peace! but now they are hid from thine eyes*).

Saints should have the knowledge and wisdom of God since our God is a God of knowledge (**I Sam. 2:3b**). We must be perfect like our heavenly Father who loves knowledge and wisdom if we are truly the children of God (**Matt. 5:43-48**). God commands us to know Him in silence and meditation saying *"Be still, and know that I am God"* (**Ps. 46:10**).

In the holy mountain of God during the millennial reign, the earth shall be full of the knowledge of God (**Is. 11:9; Hab. 2:14**). Thus to participate in the kingdom of God and to abound in divine love, we are to increase more and more in the knowledge of God (**Phil. 1:9; Col. 1:10**) which is eternal life (**John 17:3**- *And this is life eternal, that they might know thee the only true God, and Jesus Christ, whom thou hast sent.*; **I Jn. 5:20**-*And we know that the Son of God is come, and hath given us an understanding, that we may know him that is true, and we are in him that is true, even in his Son Jesus Christ. This is the true God and eternal life*).

Divine Instruction and Authority against Falsehood

(II Cor. 10:5-6) Casting down imaginations, and every high thing that exalteth itself against the knowledge of God, and bringing into captivity every thought to the obedience of Christ; And having in a readiness to revenge all disobedience, when your obedience is fulfilled.

God clearly instructs the saints to wage war against every form of falsehood that exalts itself against the knowledge of God. These falsehood 'or lying spirit may be exhibited by false prophets, false teachers, false preachers, false miracle workers, false worship ministers, false deliverance ministers and other forms of falsehood in the church and in the society that exalts itself against the truth or knowledge of God.

This spiritual warfare involves:

(i)   Casting down all imaginations against the knowledge of God
(ii) Casting down every high thing against the knowledge of God
(iii) Bringing into captivity every thought to the obedience of Christ
(iv) Having in readiness to revenge all disobedience.

This authority which saints (especially teachers) have been given is for edification of the saints and not for their destruction **(II Cor. 10:8)** and it is perfected when our obedience in Christ Jesus is fulfilled (complete and absolute, **II Cor. 10:6**). Teachers are to wage war against every reasoning, teaching, acts, machinations and devices that are formed to subject the saints to a life of ignorance or manipulation due to falsehood and bondage.

Just like Saint Paul, it is the duty of the teachers not allow the saints to be ignorant concerning our spiritual issues, warfare and the knowledge in Christ Jesus (**I Cor. 12:1**-*Now concerning spiritual gifts, brethren, I would not have you ignorant* ; **I Thess 4:13**-*But I would not have you to be ignorant, brethren, concerning them which are asleep, that ye sorrow not, even as others which have no hope*; **Romans 11:25**-*For I would not, brethren, that ye should be ignorant of this mystery, lest ye should be wise in your own conceits; that blindness in part is happened to Israel, until the fulness of the Gentiles be come in)*

Ignorance of the being of God

Lack of knowledge or awareness of the being of God hinders us from deriving maximum benefits or blessings of God. For instance, if a parent believes that a child of about 2-3 years goes to school just to learn how to stay off the parents and give them some space and time for other things, save the parents from stress and troubles at home, help to conserve food in the house then the most important objectives and goal of the school curriculum and scheme of work for that age will not be emphasized and achieved by both parents and teachers because of the poor knowledge of the overall goal of the full school curriculum and the lukewarm approach towards it. When such a child takes national or federal examinations with other students, he fails because he is disadvantaged due to the great disservice done to him.

Similarly, poor knowledge of the fullness of God the Father, the salvation and calling, the purpose and will of God in saints, and inheritances in Christ Jesus cause us to always lose in the game of life. Also, with little knowledge of God, we rejoice and be complacent without desire for the fullness of God and we are satisfied with complacency for attainment of elementary aspects of our salvation, not mindful and neither striving for the weighty issues of godliness, love and perfection in Christ Jesus.

The consequences of not having the knowledge and wisdom of God have been discussed. Furthermore, it is still very important to consider other issues resulting from the lack of divine knowledge. Ignorance of divine knowledge affected men of old who sought God by their own efforts (**Rom. 10:2**-*For I bear them record that they have a zeal of God, but not according to knowledge.*

Rom 10:3-*For they being ignorant of God's righteousness, and going about to establish their own righteousness, have not submitted themselves unto the righteousness of God*). In our time, this ignorance of the being of God or lack of knowledge and wisdom of God:

(i) Affects our ministry and service unto God on earth even if we have the zeal for God.
(ii) Hinders our relationship with God and our understanding of the perfect will of God concerning the righteousness of God.
(iii) Compels men to establish their own righteousness.
(iv) Causes men to be rebellious, not submitting themselves unto the righteousness of God. Also, workers of iniquity and those that worship idols lack the knowledge and the wisdom of God and this explains their evil disposition in life (**Ps. 14:4; Isa. 44:17-19; I Cor. 15:34**)
(v) Makes man brutish (**Prov. 30:2-3**). Truly, it is not good that a soul should be without knowledge because the foolishness of man perverts his ways and his heart frets against the Lord (**Prov. 19:2**-*Also, that the soul be without knowledge, it is not good; and he that hasteth with his feet sinneth.* **Prov 19:3**- *The foolishness of man perverteth his way: and his heart fretteth against the LORD*).

The children of Israel had known God as God Almighty and as the God of their father Abraham but they had not known God by the name Jehovah (**Ex. 6:3**). This lack of full knowledge of God negatively affected their relationship with God (**Jn 8:19**-*Then said they unto him, Where is thy Father? Jesus answered, Ye neither know me, nor my Father: if ye had known me, ye should have known my Father also*). Similarly, many saints do not have in–depth knowledge of the being of God, His attributes and personality. This little knowledge of God hampers their intimate relationship with God and the realization and actualization of their full potentials in Christ Jesus.

King Ahab, though wicked, knew God to be gracious, merciful, full of compassion, slow to anger, ready to pardon (**Neh. 9:17b**) and does not despise a broken spirit and a broken and contrite heart (**Ps. 51:17**). He humbled himself in sack cloth and ashes, fasted and prayed to God and God heard and answered him (**I King 21:28-29**). Also, the centurion had a revelation of the hierarchy and authority of Christ (**Lk.7:1-10**). He realized his unworthiness to have our Lord come unto him in his house and received the healing of his beloved servant through this realization. What about the Syrophoenician woman?

In peculiar instances God blessed persons, for instance King Cyrus, outside the commonwealth of Israel whom he had anointed and designated to deliver his chosen people (**Is. 45:1-13**) or to punish them for their sins, even when the messenger has not known God. (**Is. 45:4-5**). Yet in each instance, the sole purpose of this divine errand is that the messenger may know that Jehovah is the Lord and there is none else. In some of these errands, the messengers may misconstrue the victory over Israel to be of their own might thus incurring the wrath of God.

Many saints have neither known God nor understood that he is the omniscient, omnipresent and omnipotent one and the sovereign owner and creator of the universe and there is none to be compared to him (**Is. 12:28**). This lack of divine knowledge is a source of great fear amongst the saints. When one does not know and understand God, he lives a sinful life (**Jer. 5:5**) and the fear and love of the Lord is not in his heart (**I Jn. 3:6**). Lack of knowledge of God causes men to persecute the saints (**Jn 16:3**-*And these things will they do unto you, because they have not known the Father, nor me*).

All blessings and riches are encompassed in wisdom and knowledge of God (**Rom. 11:33**-*O the depth of the riches both of the wisdom and knowledge of God! how unsearchable are his judgments, and his ways past finding out!*). Spiritual things, especially knowledge and wisdom of God are taught and revealed by the Spirit of God; for the Spirit searches (understands) all things even the deep things of God (**I Cor. 2:9-16**). It is very pertinent for saints to have the wisdom of God for "If thou be wise, thou shall be wise for thyself; but if thou scornest, thou alone shall bear it". (**Prov. 9:12**).

Being known of God

Ps 139:1-O LORD, thou hast searched me, and known me.
Ps 139:2- Thou knowest my downsitting and mine uprising, thou understandest my thought afar off.
Ps 139:3-Thou compassest my path and my lying down, and art acquainted with all my ways.
Ps 139:4- For there is not a word in my tongue, but, lo, O LORD, thou knowest it altogether.
Ps 139:5- Thou hast beset me behind and before, and laid thine hand upon me.
Ps 139:6-Such knowledge is too wonderful for me; it is high, I cannot attain unto it.
Ps 139:7- Whither shall I go from thy spirit? or whither shall I flee from thy presence?

It is a thing of exceeding joy and a very important aspect in life to be known by the Most High who rules all creation from eternity to eternity. God uses different strategies or trials including adversities to make known the heart of man if he is of God (Ps 31:7 I will be glad and rejoice in thy mercy: for thou hast considered my trouble; thou hast known my soul in adversities; Deut. 8:2: O Lord, Thou has searched me and known me (Ps. 139:1) Being known by God implies that the saint:

a.   Has a good standing, goodwill and impressive records before God (of worship, sacrifices, services, prayers etc.) that makes him very acceptable in the presence of God (**Ex.33: 12-17**).

b.   Has an intimate relationship, an understanding or covenant that makes God to know him and accord him respect and everlasting promises as well (**Gen. 22:12b**-*for now I know that thou fearest God, seeing thou hast not withheld thy son, thine only son from me*).

c. Possesses distinct qualities and attributes which are of God (holiness, righteousness, faith, love, wisdom etc.) which are pleasing unto God that endears him to God at all times (**Job 1:.8**-*And the LORD said unto Satan, Hast thou considered my servant Job, that there is none like him in the earth, a perfect and an upright man, one that feareth God, and escheweth evil?*)

d. Has been thoroughly searched (or examined) and his heart is found to be perfect or blameless before God and seeks after God always (**Ps. 139:1-2**)

e. Has profound good works and his name has been written down in the chronicles/annals of heavens (**Acts. 10:4**-*And when he looked on him, he was afraid, and said, What is it, Lord? And he said unto him, Thy prayers and thine alms are come up for a memorial before God*; **Rev. 2-3**)

f. Has deep consciousness of God that makes him exhibit a godly lifestyle (without guile or deceit) known to God (**Jn. 1:47-49**).

g. Has developed the mind of God in such a way that God knows his thought, his words before they come out of his mouth and his plans, tendencies and things that he can never do or say (**Gen. 18:19**- *For I know him, that he will command his children and his household after him, and they shall keep the way of the LORD, to do justice and judgment; that the LORD may bring upon Abraham that which he hath spoken of him).*

The sole condition to be known by God is to love God with all your heart, soul and might (**Deut. 6:5; I Cor. 8:3**). This condition presupposes that before you love someone, you should have known his being, character, and attributes. So also, before saint can truly love God whole heartedly, it means he must have searched and have in-depth knowledge of God for such divine love to develop, manifest and be sustained. The saint must know God, for him to be known of God (**Gal. 4:9**). Every man should strive to be known by God for good and constantly pray in addition that God should also know his children even

DIVINE WISDOM AND KNOWLEDGE

from the womb (**Jer. 1:5**-*Before I formed thee in the belly I knew thee; and before thou camest forth out of the womb I sanctified thee, and I ordained thee a prophet unto the nations*).

It is absolutely important to be known by God for it will be a great disappointment for a supposed man of God to be told by God that He does not know him (**Matt 25:12**-*But he answered and said, Verily I say unto you, I know you not* **Lk 13:25** *When once the master of the house is risen up, and hath shut to the door, and ye begin to stand without, and to knock at the door, saying, Lord, Lord, open unto us; and he shall answer and say unto you, I know you not whence ye are:* **Lk 13:26** *Then shall ye begin to say, We have eaten and drunk in thy presence, and thou hast taught in our streets.* **Lk 13:27** *But he shall say, I tell you, I know you not whence ye are; depart from me, all ye workers of iniquity*.). It is a fact that God knows his saints so let no saint be in any doubt about his stance with God (**II Tim 2:19**-*Nevertheless the foundation of God standeth sure, having this seal, The Lord knoweth them that are his. And, Let every one that nameth the name of Christ depart from iniquity*).

It is very necessary to express the importance of knowing God as it saves men from the wrath of God. It is very expedient that men should know God intimately even if it will amount to the use of all available means and resources to teach divine knowledge to ensure intimate relationship and continual presence of God. The scripture in **II King 17:25-28** illustrates the wrath upon the inhabitants of the land of Israel as a result of lack of fear of God or lack of knowledge of God and the remedy by the people.

II Ki 17:25 -28-And so it was at the beginning of their dwelling there, that they feared not the LORD: therefore the LORD sent lions among them, which slew some of them.

Wherefore they spake to the king of Assyria, saying, The nations which thou hast removed, and placed in the cities of Samaria, know not the manner of the God of the land: therefore he hath sent lions among them, and, behold, they slay them, because they know not the manner of the God of the land.

Then the king of Assyria commanded, saying, Carry thither one of the priests whom ye brought from thence; and let them go and dwell there, and let him teach them the manner of the God of the land. Then one of the priests whom they had carried away from Samaria came and dwelt in Bethel, and taught them how they should fear the LORD.

Also this Bible passage teaches us to know God and strictly follow the divine pattern or manner which God prescribes and requires in his service and worship. He had strictly warned Moses to keep to the pattern which were revealed to him on the mount (**Ex. 25:40; Heb. 8:15**). Everyone that adhered to the pattern of God, as Elijah did in offer of burnt sacrifice, will always have the backing of heaven (**I King 18:29-40**).

Glorious vision of God

nowledge of God is greatly enhanced when one has as special and personal heavenly encounter with God. Here, the saint beholds an open heaven with a glorious vision of the Most High seated on throne in his beauty of holiness, awesomeness and majesty. By this heavenly encounter with God, man gets a first-hand revelation of God that is incontrovertible and indelible in his spirit. This heavenly encounter with God is enabled by the fullness of the Spirit of God in man. The Holy Spirit reveals God in the fullness of his glory to man which entirely changes the consciousness and perception of man about the perfection and excellencies of God and clearly portrays the utter depravity and worthlessness of man. This glorious revelation will assuredly show that there is none besides Him- no opposition and no contention.

Few examples of some saints that had glorious revelation of God such as Moses (**Exodus 33**), Daniel (**Daniel 10**), Isaiah (**Isaiah 6**), Ezekiel (**Eze. 1**), Job (**Job 45:5**), David (**Psalm 93, 96**), Paul (**II Cor. 12:1-12**), John (**Rev. 9**) and Stephen (**Act 7:55-56**) were extra-ordinary in manifesting divine attributes.

These saints had higher levels of revelations of God, deeper understanding of the scriptures in accordance with the perfect will of God and outstanding experiential knowledge of God. Their expositions on the law and prophets especially that of Paul, are very insightful and profound. Similarly, a cursory consideration of the mandatory nature of tithes in church will show that it was a divine way of setting up a good sustainable social security system and food security system that will cater for the poor, needy, orphans, widows, strangers, the tithers, their families and neighbours, and all categories of Levites (serving and retired){*Mal 3:10-Bring ye all the tithes into the storehouse, that there may be **meat in*** *mine house, and prove me now herewith, saith the LORD of hosts, if I will not open you the windows of heaven, and pour you out a blessing,* that *there shall* not *be room* enough *to receive it;* **Deut 14:22-***Thou shalt truly tithe all the increase of thy seed, that the field bringeth forth year by year.* **Deut 14:23-***And thou shalt eat before the LORD thy God, in the place which he shall choose to place his name there, the tithe of thy corn, of thy wine, and of thine oil, and the firstlings of thy herds and of thy flocks; that thou mayest learn to fear the LORD thy God always.* **Deut 14:24-***And if the way be too long for thee, so that thou art not able to carry it; or if the place be too far from thee, which the LORD thy God shall choose to set his name there, when the LORD thy God hath blessed thee:* **Deut 14:25-***Then shalt thou turn it into money, and bind up the money in thine hand, and shalt go unto the place which the LORD thy God shall choose:* **Deut 14:26-***And thou shalt bestow that money for whatsoever thy soul lusteth after, for oxen, or for sheep, or for wine, or for strong drink, or for whatsoever thy soul desireth: and thou shalt eat there before the LORD thy God, and thou shalt rejoice, thou, and thine household,* **Deut 14:27-***And the Levite that is within thy gates; thou shalt not forsake him; for he hath no part nor inheritance with thee.* **Deut 14:28-***At the end of three years thou shalt bring forth all the tithe of thine increase the same year, and shalt lay it up within thy gates:* **Deut 14:29-***And the Levite, (because he hath no part nor inheritance with thee,) and the stranger, and the fatherless, and the widow, which are within thy gates, shall come, and shall eat and be satisfied; that the LORD thy God may bless thee in all the work of thine hand which thou doest}.*

Misuse of tithes, lack of appropriate prayers on the tithes and first fruits by saints (Deut. 26:10-19), non-adherence to the essence of tithing and lack of strict compliance to and the fulfillment of the will of God concerning the laws of tithes prevent the saints, the church and the society from deriving maximum benefits on tithes and divine blessings. Despite the amount of preaching on tithing and the amount of tithes brought before God, as long as it is not utilized according to the perfect will of God, it profits us little or nothing as the yearnings and desires of the scripturally specified groups of persons are not met. Therefore, saints should ensure that the food and social security system should be sustained amongst saints in the church and the society, thus checking some societal ills that would have resulted from anger, anxiety, frustration and depression.

The mind of God (the mind of Christ) (1COR. 2:9-16)

Having the prescribed requirements of **Phil.2:2-8** help us to attain the mind of God or the mind of Christ that is described in **1Cor.2:9-16**. We have the mind of Christ because we have the wisdom and knowledge of God that is revealed and taught by the Spirit of God.

I Cor 2:9-But as it is written, Eye hath not seen, nor ear heard, neither have entered into the heart of man, the things which God hath prepared for them that love him. I Cor 2:10-But God hath revealed them unto us by his Spirit: for the Spirit searcheth all things, yea, the deep things of God. I Cor 2:11-For what man knoweth the things of a man, save the spirit of man which is in him? even so the things of God knoweth no man, but the Spirit of God. I Cor 2:12-Now we have received, not the spirit of the world, but the spirit which is of God; that we might know the things that are freely given to us of God. I Cor 2:13-Which things also we speak, not in the words which man's wisdom teacheth, but which the Holy Ghost teacheth; comparing spiritual things with spiritual. I Cor 2:14-But the natural man receiveth not the things of the Spirit of God: for they are foolishness unto him: neither can he know them, because they are spiritually discerned. I Cor 2:15-But he that is spiritual judgeth all things, yet he himself is judged of no man. I Cor 2:16-For who hath known the mind of the Lord, that he may instruct him? But we have the mind of Christ.

The mind of God is unsearchable and no man can discern it. It is far above the understanding or perception of any man to know the mind of God. Thus it is impossible for man's eye to see, man's ear to hear and neither does it enter into the heart of man, to know and understand the things which God have prepared for them that love him (1Cor.2:9). These things can only be perceived by having the mind of God. The possession of the mind of God ensures the reception of divine revelation to each man through the Spirit of God (**1Cor.2:10**). It is only the Spirit of God that understands and searches all things, even the deep things of God (**I Cor 2: 11**). Similarly, the spirit of man knows things (his aspiration, will, passions, proclivities, belief, histories, fears, desires, secrets etc.) of a man.

God gave us His Spirit that the saints might know all things that are freely given to us of God (**1Cor.2:12**). The Spirit of God regenerates us and makes us to appreciate and have the mind of God by attuning our minds to be in union with the mind of God. The saints no longer view or perceive things or issues according to human reasoning or feeling but only to that of God (**Is.55:8-9**). The Spirit of God makes us to understand the knowledge and wisdom of God (**1Cor.2:13**). By this knowledge and wisdom of God, saints readily appreciate and accept spiritual truths and counsels, and also understand spiritual things and manifestations which appear as foolishness unto the natural man (**1Cor.2: 14**). The spiritual man assesses and judges all things, for he has the mind of God and knows the mind of God by the Spirit of God in him (**1Cor.2:15-16**).

Hindrances to Divine Wisdom and Knowledge

in is the main hindrance to divine wisdom and knowledge. Sin hinders good and intimate communion with God (**Jer 5:25**-*Your iniquities have turned away these things, and your sins have withholden good things from you; Is. 59*). Hatred and sin barred communication and understanding between our Lord Jesus Christ and Jews (**Jn.8:43-44**) for them to hear and receive wisdom and knowledge. People of God communicate freely and understand the word of God (**John 8:47**) but those that are not of God do not understand nor hear the word of God neither do they communicate freely with children of God instead they misunderstand and misrepresent what they hear and cause havoc in the society. Sin also affected the communication and good relationship between our Lord Jesus Christ and God the father (**Matt. 27:45-46**)

Spirit of error: The evil spirit that possesses any man manifests itself by fighting against the knowledge of God (*We are of God: he that knoweth God heareth us, and he that is not of God heareth not us. Hereby know ye the spirit of truth, and the spirit of error l John 4:6*).

*An unjust man is an abomination to the just: and he that is upright in the way is abomination to the wicked. (**Prov 29:27**)*

Part VII

Conclusions

ivine wisdom and knowledge is priceless and of inestimable value, they should not be given to wicked men, fools and reprobates (**Matt, 7:6**), lest they trample on them with their feet and turn again and rend you.

Caution on Quest of Knowledge

It has always been man's ultimate desire to be like God i.e. having all the attributes and character of God, most importantly to be wise *(Gen.3:5 - For God doth know that in the day ye eat thereof, then your eyes shall be opened, and ye shall be as gods, knowing good and evil)*. The desire for knowledge, not in consonance with the will of God may be a source of temptation. It also makes one to be presumptuous without seeking the guidance and the will of God in all matters.

This desire of man to be like God maybe intrinsic because God created us in his own image and likeness even though we fell short of his glory. Overzealous pursuit of knowledge outside God's plan (in Christ Jesus) leads to much sorrow and weariness of the flesh even destruction. *(Eccl.1:17-And I gave my heart to know wisdom, and to know madness and folly: I perceived that this also is vexation of spirit. Eccl. 1:18-For in much wisdom is much grief: and he that increaseth knowledge increaseth sorrow; Eccl 12:12-And further, by these, my son, be admonished: of making many books there is no end; and much study is a weariness of the flesh).*

Much knowledge (carnal) may result in pride and presumption (*I Cor.8:1. Now as touching things offered unto idols, we know that we all have knowledge. Knowledge puffeth up, but charity edifieth).*

Much knowledge, especially human knowledge may become a fear and a hindrance to growth and development, instead of a help to us. For instance, business experts who are imbued with much theoretical knowledge do not readily establish business outfits/firms probably due to their deep awareness of risks in investments in unpredictable environment that is diametrically opposing to the optimum environment in business books.

We should seek knowledge with humility and meekness according to God's will and plan devoid of evil motives. Remember that God is unsearchable *(Ps. 145:3-Great is the LORD, and greatly to be praised; and his greatness is unsearchable; Eccl 8:17-Then I beheld all the work of God, that a man cannot find out the work that is done under the sun: because though a man labour to seek it out, yet he shall not find it; yea further; though a wise man think to know it, yet shall he not be able to find it ; Rom.11:33. O the depth of the riches both of the wisdom and knowledge of God! how unsearchable are his judgments, and his ways past finding out!).*

Withheld Divine wisdom, understanding and knowledge

Actually, at some instances, knowledge may be withheld from man according to God's definite purpose: (a) Adam and Eve were warned against the tree of knowledge of good and evil (*Gen.2:17. But of the tree of the knowledge of good and evil, thou shalt not eat of it: for in the day that thou eatest thereof thou shalt surely die);* (b) While in serious discussion recognition or knowledge of resurrected Christ was withheld from the two disciples in Emmaus *(Lk. 24:25-31).* (c) The understanding of revelation and identification of the betrayer was withheld from the disciples even though our Lord mentioned him (*Jn.13:18-I speak not of you all: I know whom I have chosen: but that the scripture may be fulfilled, He that eateth bread with me hath lifted up his heel against me).*

In our walk with God, full knowledge of divine revelations through dreams, visions, prophecies, intuition, scriptures, or angelic visitations may elude us due to our spiritual immaturity, defilement, poor prayer life, not seeking the guidance of the Holy Spirit and lack of spiritual understanding and interpretation of the figures and symbolisms used in the revelations. Other Bible citations indicating that knowledge and understanding may be withheld according to divine plan and purpose until the appointed time are:

Mat 12:16 And charged them that they should not make him known:

Mat 16:20 Then charged he his disciples that they should tell no man that he was Jesus the Christ.

Mat 17:9 And as they came down from the mountain, Jesus charged them, saying, Tell the vision to no man, until the Son of man be risen again from the dead.

Jn. **16:12**- *I have yet many things to say unto you, but ye cannot bear them now;*

I Cor.13:12 -For now we see through a glass, darkly; but then face to face: now I know in part; but then shall I know even as also I am known;

Eph. **3:5**-*Which in other ages was not made known unto the sons of men, as it is now revealed unto his holy apostles and prophets by the Spirit;*

I Jn.3:2-*Beloved, now are we the sons of God, and it doth not yet appear what we shall be: but we know that, when he shall appear, we shall be like him; for we shall see him as he is;*

Deut.29:29.-*The secret things belong unto the LORD our God: but those things which are revealed belong unto us and to our children for ever, that we may do all the words of this law;*

Prov.25:2. *It is the glory of God to conceal a thing: but the honour of kings is to search out a matter;*

Dan.12:9. *And he said, Go thy way, Daniel: for the words are closed up and sealed till the time of the end; (cf II Cor 12:2-4).*

Rev 10:4 *And when the seven thunders had uttered their voices, I was about to write: and I heard a voice from heaven saying unto me, Seal up those things which the seven thunders uttered, and write them not).*

Caution on wickedness
with Divine Wisdom

In order not to incur the wrath of God, wisdom should not be used to invent evil, devise evil machinations, enhance wickedness (sinfulness) or hold the truth in unrighteousness (*Rom.1:18-For the wrath of God is revealed from heaven against all ungodliness and unrighteousness of men, who hold the truth in unrighteousness*). Wise men should not take bribe (gifts) as gifts blind them and cause them to err (*Deut. 16:19. Thou shalt not wrest judgment; thou shalt not respect persons, neither take a gift: for a gift doth blind the eyes of the wise, and pervert the words of the righteous*).

Furthermore, pride corrupts and debases man (*Eze.28:17- Thine heart was lifted up because of thy beauty, thou hast corrupted thy wisdom by reason of thy brightness: I will cast thee to the ground, I will lay thee before kings, that they may behold thee*); Oppression causes man to lose his mind (reasoning) and bribe destroys his heart (affection, passion or love, and bowels of mercies (*Eccl.7:7-Surely oppression maketh a wise man mad; and a gift destroyeth the heart*); Also adultery and strong drinks affects our emotions and corrupt wisdom and knowledge (*Hos. 4:11. Whoredom and wine and new wine take away the heart*).

We know that where the Spirit of God is, there is liberty (*II Cor. 3:17*), therefore divine wisdom and knowledge like every other spiritual gift is given to man to set people free from bondage, oppression, power of darkness, sickness and poverty not the contraries (*Lk. 4:18-The Spirit of the Lord is upon me, because he hath anointed me to preach the gospel to the poor; he hath sent me to heal the brokenhearted, to preach deliverance to the captives, and recovering of sight to the blind, to set at liberty them that are bruised, Luk 4:19-To preach the acceptable year of the Lord*).

Caution on Misuse of Divine Wisdom and Knowledge

God's given wisdom and blessings should not be used (i) to undermine God's works and creation. (ii) to leak God's secret or betray God's people for Balaam's lucre or Iscariot's lust. (iii) to counsel evil men on how to perpetuate their evils, their sinful habits or to overcome the righteous ones. Men have become nothing and have sold off their ministries and work of God for personal gain, by operating their gifts without love (**I Cor. 13:2**).

Do not leak God's secrets or revelations to the hypocrites (unbelievers as such act does not profit God's work or his people in anyway. Misuse of talents or gifts such as (i) beauty (ii) status in the church or society (iii) money (iv) power or authority (v) gifts of the Holy Spirit without the love of God should be avoided by wise men lest your talent becomes corrupted and confounded.

Misuse of talents is seen in ill-advised policy formulations in the society, spurious and visionless projects and ventures. It also manifests in scams and lottery, organized crimes and crises, false doctrines especially the teachings of humanism, exploitation of women, children, poor workers, and men. The blessings of God may be misused by putting people in bondage, slavery, ignorance, manipulative philosophies and traditions of men, and studies of psychology (fear, hypnotism, emotions, psyche, aspirations, etc.). Misuse of children's prayer or prayers of saints for ungodly enrichments and misuse of authority for carnal marriage match-making are all against God's will.

When the misuse of wisdom persists, it results in glory of God departing from such an individual or group and possession of such individual by an evil spirit. Misuse or abuse of divine talents by any recipient amounts to treachery and rebellion. Those that are sincere and god-fearing need not fear any condemnation; for the Holy Spirit will not let them fail or let any saint misuse Him or His gift or even blaspheme against Him, the Holy Spirit.

Caution against falling from divine glory

One can fall short of the glory of God though endowed with gifts of wisdom and knowledge. Sin in its diverse nature of lust of the eye, lust of the flesh and pride of life makes a saint to lose faith in God, err and fall from the glory of God (I Jn 2:16; Gal 5:22-23). King Solomon though endowed with exceeding great wisdom and knowledge backslidded and fell from the glory of God (**Deut 17:16-18, I King 10: 24- 29; I King 11:1-13**) by:

- Greatly multiplying riches (silver and gold) thereby gradually putting his trust in rich instead of God
- Greatly multiplying horses, horsemen and chariots i.e. building a formidable army with weapons, gradually eroding his trust in God (I King 10) and trusting more in his army.
- Greatly multiplying wives and loved strange women of countries which the Lord God commanded them not to go into. These wives turned away his heart from God and he went after other gods (**I King 11:1-5**)
- Doing evil in the sight of the Lord by building high places unto other gods, burning incense, committing abominations before these gods and sacrificing unto them. (**1 King 11:6-10**)
- Disobeying the commands and warning of God not to go after other gods and forsaking the covenants of God with himself and his forebears. (**I King 11 :11**)

God was angry with Solomon, because his heart was turned from the Lord God of Israel, so he chastened him.

Conditions that Enhance Mental Development

There are certain foods and conditions that enhance good mental development, creativity and well-being of men. Some of these requirements are: foods that boost memory; good food, deep breathing of fresh air, clean drinking water, fruits, vitamins; calmness or quietness of spirit; freedom of spirit; leading of the Holy spirit; solitude; conducive living environment; love and harmony with God and man; avoidance of drugs especially drugs that works against the proper functions of the body systems and the mind; exercises (physical, mental and spiritual); rest, relaxation and sleep; constant reading/studying even learning new specialties help to develop the mind.

Conspiracy against Men of Wisdom

Wise men exhibit certain traits or characteristics that make them outstanding in professional disciplines or endeavours of life. They are men of (i) integrity (ii) great vision (iii) excellence (iv) great faith (v) hard work and perseverance (vi) creativity or imagination (vii) great intellect (viii) great concern to humanity and (ix) innovation. Do not think or be deceived that men will always cherish men of virtue or excellence, instead they will envy, hate and always conspire to destroy and hinder them as well as their visions and destinies (**Gen. 37; Matt. 26; Dan. 6**).

Also, it is not everyone that is willing or happy to marry a virtuous woman (Elimelech's kinsman in **Ruth 4:1-15**) even Nabal that married Abigail did not really understand and appreciate her value or virtues (**I Sam.25**). For these conspiracies, men of wisdom must wholly abide in Christ for the zeal of the Lord to preserve them through trials and attacks of the enemies and accomplish the will of God in them.

In life for a man to attain eexcellency in divine wisdom and knowledge, he has to understand that every divine gift(s) has its trials, discipline, price and sacrifices that must be paid in accordance with perfect will of God. Please undertake this divine task of acquiring and increasing in the wisdom and knowledge of God to the glory of God and may the good Lord strengthen you immensely. Amen.

Conclusion

As wise children of God we should not envy or fret ourselves because of the wicked/fool (*Ps. 37:1. Fret not thyself because of evildoers, neither be thou envious against the workers of iniquity*). God reveals secrets even deep secrets of heaven to whom He delights in. We should be mindful of whom we take pieces of advice. We must make sure that the adviser or counselor is wise, knowledgeable and God-fearing since iron sharpeneth iron (*Prov.27:17 Iron sharpeneth iron; so a man sharpeneth the countenance of his friend*). Friendship with wise saints has to be planned for, sought after, cultivated, nurtured and developed constantly all through one's life.

Beware of fools, wicked counselors, charlatans, hypocrites, and evil men who are always ready and willing to offer evil counsels. Avoid them! Do not seek their evil counsel nor adhere to their instructions (*Prov19:27 -Cease, my son, to hear the instruction that causeth to err from the words of knowledge*).

A fool is known by his/her conduct, his words and body language therefore, observe closely his words, thoughts and actions whether they are in consonance with the word of God (*Eccl.10:3- Yea also, when he that is a fool walketh by the way, his wisdom faileth him, and he saith to everyone that he is a fool; Matt 7: 16- Ye shall know them by their fruits. Do men gather grapes of thorns, or figs of thistles? Mat 7:17 Even so every good tree bringeth forth good fruit; but a corrupt tree bringeth forth evil fruit*).

The fruit of the wicked is sin (*Prov. 10:16-The labour of the righteous tendeth to life: the fruit of the wicked to sin*). Blessed are you if you do not have evil (ungodly) counselors (*Ps 1:1 Blessed is the man that walketh not in the counsel of the ungodly, nor standeth in the way of sinners, nor sitteth in the seat of the scornful*). You have nothing to learn or gain from an evil man because bad company or evil association corrupts (defiles) your spirit, soul and body (**I Cor 15:33**-*Be not deceived: evil communications corrupt good manners*).

Knowing, therefore, the consequences of the sin and of foolishness (i.e. lack of knowledge) as we have discussed previously, one cannot afford to remain foolish. Therefore, walk circumspectly as wise men in all your conversations, but not as fools. Re-affirm your faith in Christ Jesus or accept our Lord Jesus Christ as your Savior and God. Be wise and knowledgeable! God is the perfect counselor and mentor for persons poised for excellence. So constantly focus on God and He will bring teachers to teach you at different stages of your life.

Live life to its fullest; do not be dismayed by prevalence of foolishness in the society since you have Christ in you as the fullness of God! *(Eccl.2:24. There is nothing better for a man, than that he should eat and drink, and that he should make his soul enjoy good in his labour. This also I saw, that it was from the hand of God; Eccl.5:18- Behold that which I have seen: it is good and comely for one to eat and to drink, and to enjoy the good of all his labour that he taketh under the sun all the days of his life, which God giveth him: for it is his portion.* Happy is the man that findeth wisdom *(Prov. 3:13. Happy is the man that findeth wisdom, and the man that getteth understanding).*

Finally, I thank God for giving us the grace to navigate the way of wisdom *(Prov. 4: 11, 18 -I have taught thee in the way of wisdom; I have led thee in right paths, Prov. 4:18 But the path of the just is as the shining light, that shineth more and more unto the perfect day).* I pray that you may

- continually walk in the way of good men;
- keep the paths of the righteous *(Prov. 2:20 That thou mayest walk in the way of good men, and keep the paths of the righteous)*
- be wiser than your enemies, peers, teachers and the ancient; and
- shine as the brightness of the firmament in Jesus Christ name, Amen. *(Dan.12:3a – (And they that be wise shall shine as the brightness of the firmament). And they that turn many to righteousness as the stars for ever and ever).*

Epilogue on Divine Wisdom and Knowledge

A study on the final word on discourse (**Eccl. 12:13**), prayer (**II Cor. 13:11, 14**), command or advice (**Phil. 4:8**) in the scriptures seem to show the conclusion of the treatise or the concise summary of the book which should be committed to one's memory. Final words are similar to last words or final warning of a loved one that is departing to another place or transiting to eternity and should not be toyed with.

Lastly, I will conclude with the words of: *Rev 22:11-He that is unjust, let him be unjust still: and he which is filthy, let him be filthy still: and he that is righteous, let him be righteous still: and he that is holy, let him be holy still. Rev 22:12-And, behold, I come quickly; and my reward is with me, to give every man according as his work shall be.*

I pray God to give you the ear, will and the heart to receive, accept and put to use the wisdom and knowledge of God unlike those that gnashed their teeth and stopped their ears that they may not hear the narration and exposition of the scriptures in order to acquire wisdom and knowledge of God (*Acts.7:54-60*).

Foolishness is exciting and pleasurable to the fool when someone else is paying for the folly and its outcome.

Printed in the United States
By Bookmasters